Best Poems of 1966

BEST POEMS
of 1966

BORESTONE MOUNTAIN
POETRY AWARDS
1967

*A Compilation of Original Poetry
published in
Magazines of the English-speaking World
in 1966*

NINETEENTH ANNUAL ISSUE

VOLUME XIX

PACIFIC BOOKS, PUBLISHERS • PALO ALTO, CALIFORNIA

1967

PACIFIC BOOKS, PUBLISHERS
Palo Alto, California

© 1967 by Borestone Mountain Poetry Awards
Printed in the United States of America
Library of Congress Catalog Card Number: 49-49262

ANNOUNCEMENT OF AWARDS AND ACKNOWLEDGMENTS

Borestone Mountain Poetry Awards presents in this nineteenth volume a selection of poems originally published in magazines throughout the English-speaking world in 1966. Three hundred and thirty-two poems from over one hundred magazines were presented by our reading staff for consideration. In accordance with our long-standing procedure, the recommended poems were presented for final selections with the names of the poets and publications deleted since no distribution between recognized poets and newcomers is intended. There is also no intention to distribute the results geographically or between the well-known and the smaller magazines. Translations and poems of over one hundred lines are not considered.

Michael Van Walleghen received the first award of $300 for his poem "The Permanence of Witches." The second award of $200 goes to Charles Causley for his poem "By St Thomas Water," and the third award of $100 to Norman Friedman for "Love Poem."

The editors wish to recognize the loyal services of Gertrude Claytor, who is retiring from the editorial board this year. She has devoted fourteen years of continuous service to the work of presenting the annual selections. The editors also wish to express their appreciation for the splendid cooperation of the magazines that publish poetry, and we gratefully acknowledge permission to reprint these selected poems from the magazines, publishers, and authors owning the copyrights. Poems requiring special acknowledgments and notes are listed below.

THE EDITORS

LIONEL STEVENSON, *Chairman*   HILDEGARDE FLANNER
HOWARD SERGEANT   GERTRUDE CLAYTOR
  British Commonwealth Magazines   FRANCES MINTURN HOWARD
  (except Canada)   GEMMA D'AURIA
WADDELL AUSTIN, *Managing Editor*

Alistair Campbell's poem "Why Don't You Talk to Me?" originally printed in *Poetry Australia,* April 1966, was reprinted in a collection of his verse, *Blue Rain,* by the Wai-Te-ata Press, Wellington, New Zealand.

CONTENTS

Best Poems of 1966

THE PERMANENCE OF WITCHES

The moon
stars and weather
happen as they always have,
and between old Salem
where the pale women
burned like leaves
and this midwestern town,
the ash of dark reality
has sifted, settled down
and become the neighborhood
at suppertime,
the wives we take to bed.
And I think
those trivial lives
that gathered once
among the ferns,
among the oaks
that scattered near the sea
at Salem,
were not more evil than our own,
but neither could the men
have better understood
what drives a woman
not to love.

Tonight, in black,
on a broomstick riding,
the witch the watcher
the spiteful other
coasts out and out
along the frigid edges of her life
and these abandoned shapes,
these faithful wives we love
and learn to hate,
this girl that moans
beneath me, far away,
this body burned
and sick to death
of burning, turns
in the pale half-light,
in the fires
hissing near the sea
at Salem.

MICHAEL VAN WALLEGHEN

BY ST THOMAS WATER

By St Thomas Water
Where the river is thin
We looked for a jam-jar
To catch the quick fish in.
Through St Thomas Church-yard
Jessie and I ran
The day we took the jam-pot
Off the dead man.

On the scuffed tombstone
The grey flowers fell,
Cracked was the water,
Silent the shell.
The snake for an emblem
Swirled on the slab,
Across the beach of sky the sun
Crawled like a crab.

"If we walk," said Jessie,
"Seven times round,
We shall hear a dead man
Speaking underground."
Round the stone we danced, we sang,
Watched the sun drop,
Laid our heads and listened
At the tomb-top.

Soft as the thunder
At the storm's start
I heard a voice as clear as blood,
Strong as the heart.
But what words were spoken
I can never say,
I shut my fingers round my head,
Drove them away.

4

"Jessie, what are those letters
Cut so sharp and trim
All round this holy stone
With earth up to the brim?"
Jessie traced the letters
Black as coffin-lead.
"He is not dead but sleeping,"
Slowly she said.

I looked at Jessie,
Jessie looked at me,
And our eyes in wonder
Grew wide as the sea.
Past the green and bending stones
We fled hand in hand,
Silent through the tongues of grass
To the river strand.

By the creaking cypress
We moved as soft as smoke
For fear all the people
Underneath awoke.
Over all the sleepers
We darted light as snow
In case they opened up their eyes,
Called us from below.

Many a day has faltered
Into many a year
Since the dead awoke and spoke
And we would not hear.
Waiting in the cold grass
Under a crinkled bough,
Quiet stone, cautious stone,
What do you tell me now?

CHARLES CAUSLEY

LOVE POEM

Apparently I'll never get used to the way
your intelligent body unfolds to my urgent touch
how that extravagant animal which has been asleep
all day awakens at night to gentle me
shyly and sensuously to surprise me
with the perfection of its eloquent lust.

The mathematics of seven thousand nights
somehow fail to occupy my mind
as I cast up the figures you will integrate tonight.
The millionth kiss cannot be learned
and no amount of study can tell
why the spirit multiplies as the flesh divides.

All my life it was always goodbye
goodbye for the summer goodbye
for the winter alone and departing
among the magazines and souvenirs
and the fatal precision of timetables.
But your goodbye was the cruellest

the most lonely and the most precise
equalling all the others together
as impotent little hopes were subtracted from my heart.
Until one day we turned to each other saying
hello for the fall hello for the spring
and kissed the young kiss we're kissing now.

The problem of leaving love behind was solved
in the additions of your body's wisdom
and I have heard what your lips can think
as they speak dumbly on mine
for this was the language and the axiom
you taught this inept pupil of your virginity.

Most women aren't especially beautiful
their bodies sufficient for love for babies
and for providing and surely that is sufficient.
In March the hearts of even the most ordinary people
yearn for the spring hoping for sun wondering
whether the forsythia will blossom in the snow.

Such pedantry about the arrival of flowers
is not the exclusive concern of poets then.
But even in the fall the discovery of your thighs
gives such insight as still serves around the house
to formulate your unconscious nakedness
in classic model's poses amidst trivial routines.

or in making love when your beautiful body speaks
to awaken the ears of my soul to theorems.
This contrast survives the violent perfection of summer
and weathers the extravagant repetitions of winter
because I am always young to you I am always young
and you are forever the same as you always were.

NORMAN FRIEDMAN

THE ANIMALS AT THE FAIR

Before even the glorious ferris wheel,
we wanted the animals. "Wild!
Exotic!" cried the menagerie man.
Inside, we saw the molting hawk ignore,
for the third year in a row,
boys and their sticks. The fox
caressed his cage door with a furious muzzle.
He was new, unused to noise.
We counted splinters in his nose.
The giant bat uncloaked himself, a mouse-mouth yawn
and wing-tips touching wire on either side.
One old wildcat stalked his shadow
while his eyes stood still.
When we had seen them all,
We moved to the music and wheeling lights
where people were passing each other.
Behind their fixed looks something quick walked,
jerked at the end of its chain,
then turned to cross a face again.

BETTY ADCOCK

THE PROMISE

On this fourth day of a new year I sit
in bright sunlight as I have so often
these past five years, knowing nothing I say
can take my place in your presence. I no
longer suspect my thinking of you on
sunlit mornings, sure as I am that you
read for what is said. Each of us has grown
new and busy. You've learned to hurry, and
though I'm forgetting how I still sometimes
forget to forget, which sounds cleverer
than it really is. I remember when
and where I want.

Many very long years
ago, it seems, hurried by pain and loss
I wrote you another, unmailed letter.
Rereading it a while back, slowly, I
found the pain quieted and the loss at
least shifted, like one's weight from one foot to
the other. Most of what I wrote there and
then I'd repeat today except that the
advice and warning, like all good counsel,
would be more tiresomely obvious to
you than it now is to me, who know less
about more each year.

But as I can't be
with you it is advice I want to give.
Being your father, I know full well how
apt you are to follow it, which doesn't
completely displease me. Hardheads like you
and me have what we have by being hit
with it. At worst, however, you won't need
the advantage I've had of saying you've
never been told, a slight but useful edge,
as is my willing reluctance to talk
at all. Patience, boy. No one gets through hell
in a hurry. Nor to heaven.

About
money. Walk, don't run from it. It often
strikes at quick movements of any kind. Do
not tease or disdain it. It has no sense
of humor whatsoever, and like all
powerful creatures it feeds on smaller
animals. Smaller, not weaker. If you
come to a place where you must take or be
taken by it, stand easily, smile. Smile
especially. It will then be yours. With
it you will seldom get what you want, but
you will always get what you ask for.

This
of course is true of many things. Women,
for instance, who you will discover are
exceptions to every rule except that
one. There is nothing more to say. Despite
the nervous humor which I've caused a few
people, I've made a point not to study
women. That is, the live ones. The dead ones
are a fascinating study, and I
commend them to you. Other than that you
can sometimes touch and talk with the live ones,
I know only that what you do with them
stays with you longest of anything.

10

                                    Do
not wad up things or persons unless you
intend to throw them away. Fold them and
put them where they belong. No matter what
you do, don't do with money or women,
do not ever expect miracles in
mailboxes. You will never find faith, hope,
or charity in receptacles. These
virtues come when they do from your own ten
finger-tips, and then only if you keep
telling yourself that others can't help not
being as good or bad as you are.

                                    So,
enough. By now I mistrust long letters.
It's late. The afternoon sunlight's gone down
and off the table I'm writing on. A
Sunday evening fills the gloomy places,
which always seem darker when I've had less
to say than I thought I had. Yet when I've
talked a lot I know I've told a few lies
without even meaning to. I feel I
should miss you more than I do, but each time
we visit one another there's less to
say because there's less left to miss, and this
is the way almost everything ends.

                              CARROLL ARNETT

TOLD IN THE SEED

Tonight I hear the first crickets on the hillside,
A big brown spider sits on my dictionary,
The moon is full, o, moon pulling at my tides.
I know the bees are cold tonight, the spring is uncertain,
But flowers are waiting; they have come up
From their secret seeds, no seed confused in its image
No matter how I mix them in the earth,
The worm's fragrant home.
We are strung on the same breath, and this is the secret.
We have not made the deep connection.
This acacia tree with a composition of night birds
Whispers its being, its covenant, and what cannot be said,
Told in the seed; persuaded by sun, sod, the rain and wind,
The lightning and thunder.
I hear the crickets making a song upon the hills.

SANORA BABB

CHANGING A DIAPER ON CHUCKANUT DRIVE

We are enclosed by a ring of shadowy cones
spattered with white.
Far below, the sand flat's silver glaze
reflects, a plate
of no-color, sun already gone.
The sheer layer
is sprinkled with dark sandpipers as with seed,
a random smear.
Guttural queries creak across the bay;
all else is mute.
Receding in a secrecy of blue
are islands, remote
as animals; slumbrous, elongated
ovals, oblongs
uncertainly outlined, their edges washed grey.

To select then
only the inhuman is the temptation here:
an ideal scene,
the beautiful abstracts unfurled like a peacock's tail
to shimmering grandeur,
the unfragmented sum of all its parts.
Do I take the lure?
I lean down, out, over what can only be
immediate danger,
craving totality. The cold wind urges;
I give ear.
Temporal, I am recalled by a human cry,
an exact request,
unsparing. I do not linger; but salute
the ambient Ghost.

BETH BENTLEY

THE LESSON

Four fingers and a thumb
encircle the stiff tool,
a slick, unyielding length
alien to animal softness
the squat warmth of a fist.

Like a snail her cupped hand crawls
suctioned to page and pencil,
leaking a shaky trail.
Her infant bones resist
the rigid, strike out, pull back,
dance a rebellious tango:
Nature makes a last ditch struggle.

My hand, housing hers, guides,
learning again wonder:
we trace an old cabala.
Abstraction goes eccentric,
becomes arrow, bridge or flag;

my hand reverts to paw,
unknowing, simply feeling;
while hers awakes. I feel it
break from its shell, flutter
to awareness in the cage of mine.
Together across the page
we draw toward a name.

BETH BENTLEY

SEA BITCH

Wet down
    classic primitive
commanding O sea-tidal! face!
How can I be alone: she will not let me
    be alone.
I come from the cloud-herd; the blue,
    malefic, bruises my lips.
Sand clogs mind. Coral cuts to bone.
    Blood batters toward embrace
(violent face against visored face).
    She will be known.

    She takes me
(too willingly wed
to emptying; too rushing to be shed
    of troubling in great veins).
"Bleed," she invokes, maternal breasts
    full silvery.
    "Be emptied. Come to bed."

I will not be alone.
Once soft voices linger, voices long since thrown
    to thunders without testament.
Old monarchs who fed the foam recall
how waters were stilled by songs long-sung.
    Over bed's chronicle, the harp is hung.

    "Be emptied . . . Be emptied . . ."
Like waves, the demented phrases fall.

    Possessed, I face
her face, fiercely close, and throb at sting
    of blood's jetted mindless art.
    I have no temperate heart.
    I cling
where sleep lulls: favor's private place.

Necessity, alas. She molds a mouth to feed.
    She dips in red. Her canticle is "Bleed."

SAM BRADLEY

PARADISE STREET

I said Farewell to Kitty my dear

They cut the sea, those days, as the Dutch cut diamonds,
Driving their daisy Blackballers, their dolphin packets,
Bound away from, say, Boston to any place heathen and
    scented,
Putting, by God, some spice in the eighteen hundreds.

They rounded the Horn, and be damned to whatever
    Antarctica
Sent up to snap off her sticks in the way of port weather.
The storm in the master was worse. He stumped stem to
    stern of her,
Thunder and lightning on legs, the eye of his own hurricane.

And out from the broad-beamed whalers they took their
    Nantucket
Sleigh-rides abaft the disastrous, oil-heavy right whales:
Broken like dolls when one breached beneath them, they
    drifted
To the nearest land anywhere, usually three miles down.

They were hard-looking tickets, and tough. It took the
    unsanded
To sail a ship and survive her. The crews, rib and spine, were
    shaped on
Old ways, with their hearts hammered out on Davy Jones'
    anvil—
Oak and iron, every man jack of them, oakum and pitch.

—What sounds meet you now, sweet Trades? O where do
    the cross-trees
Creak? Where's the mast-head lookout, bawling: "She
    blows! Ah, she *breaches*?"
A later gale swallowed his voice—and his life, like as not—
    and a later
Sun came up on a sea as empty as New England eyes now.

My family once harbored two captains, in a hard life much
    harder cases:
Devil Jack Brown, born John, and his brother James, known
    as Bully.
They were lava-mouthed men who seethed at the sight of
    grim awkward side-wheelers
Stinking their black way across a cinder-befouled Atlantic.

Devil Jack, the fo'c'sle said, got his name from being shipped
    up here
From Hell on consignment, but no chandler wanted the
    bundle.
"He never smoked *see*-gars a-bed, but his berth got scorched
    frequent by somethin',"
The fo'c'sle said, "and he trimmed his beard with Saint Elmo's
    Fire."

In the horse latitudes once, becalmed for a week and nigh
    boiling,
Bully Brown cussed clear through four watches, in Chinese,
    broad Scots, and Malay:
Lacking horses, or even a mule, he jettisoned ship's cook and
    bo'sun,
Picking them up, with regret, when the wind freshened half
    a day later.

They watched their world founder, those masters of sailing
    vessels,
Going down stern first, with her proud bow aimed at
    Arcturus;
And themselves, poor hulks, sargassoed, not worth the
    salvage,
Entwined in kelp, slept the Sleep by their oxidized sextants.

—What trysts for you now, sad Trades? O where do the
    wakes go
When the ships long since are hull-down and half-seas-over?
The pier-haunting girls have died inland, whose beaus, taut
    in canvas,
Bubbled lead-weighted into the ooze, past the weeping
    porpoise.

My father never shipped out, and with him our eighteen
    hundreds
Sank with all hands off Maine, while the gulls fought over
    the flotsam.
Dear God, he felt guilty, though! He once built a lovely-
    lined clipper
That scudded to Nowhere across our dining room mantel.

HARRY BROWN

AVISO

Ask me when I saw the moths collecting
In the candle—the robins hitting
Windows with a smack: it was
The day I shot the mole's
Head off as he tested
An edge of outside
(How he leapt, Nijinsky!),
Fell back and looked around:

"This keeps happening," he said
As he lifted the lid of his eye
By hand to see me standing
(Unloaded but
He was beginning to be blind)—
"And I can't see why.
In my head
Across the hole there,"
He continued,
"I hold sounds
To make men
Forget dominion—"
(His cough was obsolete.)
"You who cross us over
In the dark,
Tasting in your giddy laps
The deaths of moths and swallows—"
(—Robins?)
"Happily building corners
With breasts by Silicon,
You might remember—"

(Here his eyes enlarged
Like cannons
From the other side)
"—Even without devices
Of pure logic,
It has always been possible
Not to slay me."

So he died and left
The skin of an anchorite.

SHARON LEE BROWN

WHY DON'T YOU TALK TO ME?

Why do I post my love letters
in a hollow log?
Why put my lips to a knothole in a tree
and whisper your name?

The spiders spread their nets
and catch the sun,
and by my foot in the dry grass
ants rebuild a broken city.
Butterflies pair in the wind,
and the yellow bee,
his holsters packed with bread,
rides the blue air like a drunken cowboy.

More and more I find myself
talking to the sea.
I am alone with my footsteps.
I watch the tide recede
and I am left with miles of shining sand.

Why don't you talk to me?

ALISTAIR CAMPBELL

CONCERNING NECESSITY

It's quite true we live
in a kind of rural twilight
most of the time giving
our love to the hard dirt
of this country to the weeds
and to the difficult woods

ho we say drive the wedge
heave the axe run the hand shovel
dig the potato patch
dig the ashes dig the gravel
tickle the dyspeptic chainsaw
make it snarl once more

while the henhouse needs cleaning
and the fruitless corn to be cut
and the house is falling to pieces
the car coming apart
the boy sitting and complaining
about something everything anything

this was the world foreknown
well I had thought somehow
probably in the delusion
of that idiot thoreau
our necessity could be saved
by the things we actually have

like our extreme white birch
clasped in the hemlock's arms
and our baybreasted nuthatch
and our mountain and our stars
and really these things do serve
a little though not enough

what saves the undoubted collapse
from the far worse undoubted fear
is my coming all at once
when she is done in or footsore
or down asleep in the field
or telling a song to a child

coming and seeing her move
in some particular way
that makes me refall to love
all over for human beauty
the beauty I can't believe
right here where I live.

HAYDEN CARRUTH

SCHOOL AT FOUR O'CLOCK

At four o'clock the building enters harbour.
All day it seems that we have been at sea.
Now, having lurched through the last of the water,
We lie, stone-safe, beside the jumping quay.
The stiff waves propped against the classroom window,
The razor-coloured cliffs we never pass,
The question-mark of green coiling behind us,
Have all turned into cabbages, slates, grass.

Up the slow hill a squabble of children wanders
As silence dries the valley like a drought,
When suddenly that speechless cry is raging
Once more round these four walls to be let out.
Like playing cards the Delabole slates flutter,
The founding stone is shaken in its mine,
The faultless evening light begins to stutter
As the cry hurtles down the chimney-spine.

Packing my bag with useless bits of paper
I wonder, when the last word has been said,
If I'd prefer to find each sound was thudding
Not round the school, but just inside my head.
I watch where the street lamp with sodium finger
Touches the darkening voices as they fall.
Outside? Inside? Perhaps either condition's
Better than his who hears nothing at all.

And I recall another voice. A teacher
Long years ago, saying, *I think I know*
Where all the children come from, but the puzzle
To me is, as they grow up, where they go?
Love, wonder, marvellous hope. All these can wither
With crawling years like flowers on a stalk;
Or, to some Piper's tune, vanish for ever
As creatures murdered on a morning walk.

Though men may blow this building up with powder,
Drag its stone guts to knacker's yard, or tip,
Smash its huge heart to dust, and spread the shingle
By the strong sea, or sink it like a ship—
Listen. Through the clear shell of air the voices
Still strike like water from the mountain bed;
The cry of those who to a certain valley
Hungry and innocent came. And were not fed.

CHARLES CAUSLEY

BOY

He is in his room sulked shut. The small
pouts of his face clenched. His tears
as close to holy water as I recall
any first font shining. A boy, and fierce
in his sacrament, father-forced this two-
faced way love has. And I, who

am chain-chafed and galled as any son,
his jailor; my will, his cell;
his hot eyes, mine. "Whose will be done?"
I think, wrong as a man. Oh, very well—
I make too much of nothing much. My
will a while. A boy's tears dry

into the smudge of any jam. Time hurts,
but I am not much destiny. I am,
at best, what cries with him; at worst,
that smallest God, the keeper of one lamb
that must be made to follow. Where?
That takes more God than I am to make clear.

I'm wrong as a man is. But right as love,
and father of the man whose tears I bless
in this bud boy. May he have cried enough
when he has cried this little. I confess
I don't know my own reasons or own way.
May sons forgive the fathers they obey.

JOHN CIARDI

COMMEMORATING MICHAEL COLLINS

Michael Collins was a leader in the Irish insurrection. After a split
in the revolutionary ranks, he was killed in an ambush set by some
of his former comrades.

A woman said, "He would sit there,
Listening to songs, my mother's sheaf,
And he would charm her to regain
Songs out of note for fifty years,
(Did he remember the old songs?)
For he was of the mould of men
Who had renown in her young days,
The champions of cross-roads and field."

    (His head was like the head upon
      A coin when coins were minted well,
      An athlete passing from the games
      To take his place in citadel.)

"But once I saw a sadness come
  Upon his face, and that was strange—
  The song she sang had less of fret
  Than all the rest—a Milking Song:
(Did he remember the old songs?)
  A girl's lilt as she drew streams
  Into the pail at evening fall!
  But you would think some great defeat
  Was in his mind as she sang on."

    (Some man whom Plutarch tells about
      Heard in the cadence of a song
      The breaking of a thread, and knew
      The hold he had was not for long.)

"Only that once. All other times
The house was quiet as his face
As he sat there. The open door—
It was a sign no danger lay
Across the path of that young man
Listening, or speaking of a hope
That was made secret in a song.
Did he remember the old songs?"

       (A strategist, he left behind
        Pursuit each day and thwarted death
        To plan campaign would leave no name
        To field nor to a shrine a wreath.)

But she had seen upon his face
Something that danger could not cause
Nor she could guess: the fateful glimpse
On instant opened to the man
Summoned by history. He will know
While someone outside lilts the words
That have no fret, that he must choose
Between what forceful men will name
Desertion, but that he'll conceive
As action to bring fruitful peace.
And see (it could be) rifle raised
Against deserter who had led.

       (Who breaks into a history breaks
        Into an ambush frenzy-set,
        Where comrades turn to foes, and they
        The clasp of comradeship forget.)

"Did he remember the old songs?"
  She asks as requiem leads us on
  By quays, through streets, to burial-ground.
  I answered from my searching mind,
"His powers made him prodigy,
  But old devotions kept him close
  To what was ours; he'd not forget
  Threshold and hearthstone and old songs.
  The requiem made for divers men
  Is history; his music was
  The thing that happens, as said Finn."
"No one is left on Ireland's ground
  To hear that music," she intoned
"Since Michael Collins walks no more."

  (The citadel he entered in
    Without procession or acclaim
    And brought a history to an end,
    Setting his name 'gainst Norman name.)

PADRAIC COLUM

FOR THE CHILDREN OF TEREZIN

"The 15,000 children were assembled by the Germans and wedged into Terezin, a camp in Czechoslovakia and way-station to Auschwitz. Approximately 100 survived. Poems and drawings were found in the Terezin barracks after the war."

They smelled like grandfathers,
those children,
like *zaydeh* who died
in Prague one evening,
dignified
with candles . . .
they smelled of old thighs,
old laws, and wine
turned black as graves.

From the fragile web
of their midnight dawn
they learned
to fashion quills,
dipping the tips of their bones
into the sweet
liquid
of many dreams . . .
making small tracks
on paper
like winter birds.

They sang of butterflies
and mice,
jellied quince, fleas,
cats with yellow
fur, and blossoms
forever as the sun;
they accepted
the coloring-book of the world,
knowing only that
landscapes are bright,
that trees
have many arms,
and that corpses are green
as grass.

STANLEY COOPERMAN

THE ALBUM

Your letters still exist,
of course, wrinkled
in a glass box. . . .
but I don't remember why
they were, or how, and I see
your face through water:
like a rose
too long under the rain.

Petals turn pale
under the rain,
dissolving,
like your face losing the line
where it begins
and ends, a kind of white
mud.

What do I remember?
your teeth
biting into almonds,
your voice
biting into space,
a touch of moisture
cooling your mouth.

These flavors return
as an idea,
but what can I taste
inside my head?
It's all very peculiar
and very
damp, as though
I were trying to kiss you
through a curtain
of wet silk.

STANLEY COOPERMAN

REPORT BACK

"O dark dark dark. They all go into the dark,
The vacant interstellar spaces."—T. S. ELIOT: *East Coker*.

Galactic probe seven-thousand and four
Reports an uneventful journey, free
From any serious meteoric collisions.
Geological and radiation
Surveys are now being prepared, though our first
Instrumentation suggests little, if
Any, difficulty in setting up
The usual research apparatus.

*And looking into the void
From the far edge of our empire
We see the next galaxy
A rapidly receding
Thumb-smudge of light in a mid-
Night violet sky pierced by the
Dead-lights of a handful of planets,
Red-tinged and steady like the
Eyes of disappointed lovers,
And our perspective's gone.*

Gravity repulsion is now reduced
To a minimum, while preliminary
Spectrascopic analysis suggests
Possible vegetation, though we seem,
At present, on what is clearly a desert.

Pock-marked with small craters
To the edge of a ragged
Horizon, and long-shadowed
In what passes for a moon
On the galactic periphery,
Here is an austere beauty,
Barren, uncompromising,
Like that which must have been
Experienced by men
On the ice-caps and deserts
As they once existed on earth
Before their urbanization.
Harsh and unambiguous
It throws, as it were, a man
Into himself. Is this what
The early poets wrote about?

Our first extra-craft exploration has
Returned with specimens, one of which may
Be a new mineral. We are working
On the uranium breakdown now.
We have found, also, what appear to be
Pebbles, which suggest the action of seas,
Suggesting life, if not now, at some time.
With the spectrascopic analysis
This could prove most interesting. We will
Begin work radio-gravitation
Project immediate first light. Meanwhile,
We are now occupied with lab. work as
It is eighty hours until the next "dawn."
The darkness, as expected, is intense.

34

O the dark, the deep hard dark
Of these galactic nights!
Even the planets have set
Leaving it slab and impenetrable,
As dark and directionless
As those long nights of the soul
The ancient mystics spoke of.
Beyond there is nothing,
Nothing we have known or experienced.
It is such a dark
To be lost in which a man
Might, perhaps, find himself.

Excessive hyperwarp has set up
A fault in our auxiliary booster,
Could you contact the depot-ship asking
To send a supply-cruiser with a spare?
And, while they are at it, some playing-cards
Or a set of Galaxtopoly with
A few of the latest girlie magazines.
Anything to kill the time.

If a man could stare out
Such a darkness and endure,
In such a darkness a man
Might, perhaps, find himself,
Scoured to the quick
In the timeless sands of the void.

Anything, as I said, to kill the time.

JOHN COTTON

NOTES FOR A WEDDING ANNIVERSARY

A gift of wood is appropriate for the sixth year

1

This morning you made your bed again
and mine, the same bed.
Morning after morning
I am aging with the knowledge
that I cannot know
what you think of, adjusting
the place where I sleep,
and will over and over.

2

I have considered writing you
anonymous love letters,
fearing that my voice has grown
so familiar you no longer hear it;
fearing that I talk too much
or that you listen with one ear;
fearing that when I scream my best
there is no sound in the air,
and you have come to consider me
the universe's most accomplished maker
of amazing, silent, useless faces.

3

All this furniture; menus; policies;
calendars dark with marginalia;
three named children; doors; lamps;
how hard it is to cross a room!

4

Like the shifty creatures
in a fairy tale, we happen
on the incantations and specially
placed kisses for transforming
one another at the last possible moment.
Hag, talking bird, superb princess,
what further stunts must I perform
to get at your true and final shape?

5

Painfully, I am learning the pathos
of my own instruments, these cumbersome,
obsolete devices that I mark you with
trying to get the truth out of myself.

6

Six years in the making, dear collaborator,
wife, this should have been a love story. I'm **sorry**
but it is, it really is.

JAMES CRENNER

THE SHEEP-CHILD

Farm boys wild to couple
With anything   with soft-wooded trees
With mounds of earth   mounds
Of pine straw   will keep themselves off
Animals by legends of their own:
In the hay-tunnel dark
And dung of barns, they will
Say   I have heard tell

That in a museum in Atlanta
Way back in a corner somewhere
There's this thing that's only half
Sheep   like a woolly baby
Pickled in alcohol   because
Those things can't live   his eyes
Are open   but you can't stand to look
I heard from somebody who . . .

But this is now almost all
Gone. The boys have taken
Their own true wives in the city,
The sheep are safe in the west hill
Pasture   but we who were born there
Still are not sure. Are we,
Because we remember, remembered
In the terrible dust of museums?

Merely with his eyes, the sheep-child may
Be saying   saying
I am here, in my father's house.
I who am half of your world, came deeply
To my mother in the long grass
Of the west pasture, where she stood like moonlight
Listening for foxes. It was something like love
From another world that seized her
From behind, and she gave, not lifting her head
Out of dew, without ever looking, her best
Self to that great need. Turned loose, she dipped her face
Farther into the chill of the earth, and in a sound
Of sobbing   of something stumbling
Away, began, as she must do,
To carry me. I woke, dying,

In the summer sun of the hillside, with my eyes
Far more than human. I saw for a blazing moment
The great grassy world from both sides,
Man and beast in the round of their need,
And the hill wind stirred in my wool,
My hoof and my hand clasped each other,
I ate my one meal
Of milk, and died
Staring. From dark grass I came straight

To my father's house, whose dust
Whirls up in the halls for no reason
When no one comes   piling deep in a hellish mild corner,
And, through my immortal waters,
I meet the sun's grains eye
To eye, and they fail at my closet of glass.
Dead, I am most surely living
In the minds of farm boys: I am he who drives
Them like wolves from the hound bitch and calf
And from the chaste ewe in the wind.
They go into woods   into bean fields   they go
Deep into their known right hands. Dreaming of me,
They groan   they wait   they suffer
Themselves, they marry, they raise their kind.

JAMES DICKEY

VIPER'S BUGLOSS

The same color,
sea level or elevation:
the blue of the flame
of good gas

wrapped
in pink, a bud
the color of
an unstruck match,

fuming by roads
cut through rock
gray as rock dust,
leaves branching out,
each plant
a neat ideogram
for fire.

A different blue,
it tugs at
the driver's eye.
Biff! Whoom!
The cars pass.

A survivor of accidents,
I crawled as far away
as an island,
and on its furthest tip

found an owl's skull,
an edge of cookstove,
and the unquenchable blue
of a good gas flame.

The hemlocks testified
(handing out wisps of seaweed)
to somewhat too much
water at high tide

as did the stem—
rubbery, infinite, branching—
from a crevasse in rock.
But what it said was identical:

Survival is not a choice;
equipped, you adapt,
and death
is what keeps you alive.

RUTH FOX

DIVER

Water regards him with hard eyes
For a moment, taking blue on her green
And him, hung with clouds and weeds
In loosening levitation of his dive.

With practice arched and drawn
By what he sees, touches finger
Tips, and with a kiss is down
The blossom that she opens at his touch

To take his curving length
Inside, burning beauty from him
In phosphorous fire — form's
Deliquescence in metaphor —

Trailing comets, suns, moons, eyes
In a swath of alchemy, of poet
Plunged into his element —
Gesture and song become crystalline.

Walks a moment on shadows of fins —
Wings, the fallen, wavering
In weeds below; and hovers
Among columns of burning sun,

Almost absorbed by the dream
Of shapes he could one depth
Closer see; but thrashes up
And up to gasp ecstatic air.

In that instant made, blurred and blended
With the waves, he rises to the dock;
The once excited sea shifts, blinks,
And gives him back his weight.

MAURICE GIBBONS

A BIRD SINGS TO ESTABLISH FRONTIERS

Perhaps if we could begin some definite way.
At a country inn of the old Russian novels,
Maybe. A contrived place to establish manner.
With roles of traditional limit for distance.
I might be going back, and there would be a pause.
Late at night, while they changed the horses on your sled.
Or prepared my room. An occasion to begin.
Though not on false terms. I am not looking for love.
I have what I can manage, and too many claims.
Just a formal conversation, with no future.
But I must explain that I will probably cry.
It is important you ignore it. I am fine.
I am not interested in discussing it.
It is complicated and not amiable.
The sort of thing our arrangements provide against.
There should be a fireplace. Brandy, and some cigars.
Or cheese with warm crackers. Anything which permits
The exercise of incidental decorum:
Deferring to the other's preceding, asking
For a light. Vintages. It does not matter what.
The fireplace is to allow a different grace.
And there will be darkness above new snow outside.
Even if we agree on a late afternoon,
There would still be snow. Inside, the dining room must
Have a desolate quality; so we can talk
Without raising our voices. Finally, I hope
It is understood we are not to meet again.
And that both of us are men, so all that other
Is avoided. We can speak and preserve borders.
The tears are nothing. The real sorrow is for that
Old dream of nobility. All those gentlemen.

JACK GILBERT

IRRECONCILABLES

How to explain that on the day
we knew disease had invaded her
who had brought us into the world,
that death had cornered her like a weapon
she would not escape for long,
the winter sun spread vastly
and with utter ease
giving sharpness to each thing,
making all things stand out
as usually they don't:
a line of ships rooted like rocks,
and people in the frozen streets
free and light as the breath
that clung to them like clouds.

Along the edge of the cold sky
a strip of deep lavender ran
like a streamer in a wind
pulled by an invisible string,

and the water in the port
made over by days of cold
looked chopped but permanent, as if
the sea were chunks of bottleglass.

And everywhere surfaces
giving off the winter sun
in a sort of game of catch,
throwing at each the light
that each received, so that
the effect was a jubilation,
a juggler's feat so fast,
so intricate a trick, the full
extent of its multifarious display
escaped our eyes. But the sense
that it was there, and that
it meant not to deceive
but to reveal a joy
did not elude us.

Yet we were driving to get to her
who we feared might soon be gone.
And how were we to reconcile
exuberance with what we were about?

That a car was taking us
to the condition we call death,
that extinction could occur
when the day showed itself
in a display so bright
it seemed a game of light,
that disappearance should
make sense when all about us
objects we could not name
flared up in a cold winter sun
and shone until we had to turn
from them as from a flame,
nothing in us could reconcile,
nothing in us could explain.

ARTHUR GREGOR

THE OLD QUEEN

It is so long now I'm afraid
I don't remember very much
of how it was before I lost
him; and there were so many things
I thought I could never forget

and have forgotten them. Sometimes
I say to myself, what were they,
and I do not know. It may be,
when I am very old, even
ready to die, it will all come

back to me. I cannot hear him
speaking now, nor sing, although his
voice was his greatest beauty, so
they would tell me. But I sometimes
remember the shape of his knees,

and yet I think I never saw
them naked, and the lovely feet
he had, because he was country,
perhaps, and so going barefoot
as a child. And yet I always

remember how he sweat with love
so as I held him I found him
shining in my hands with water,
as if he had come from his house
of emerald under the sea,

leaving a mantle of silver
scales with the driftwood on the shore,
only to show me he was still
a prince, and how the spell that held
him, broke for a little kindness.

SUZANNE GROSS

AT SHOREHAM

for Lynn

Nightfall and my hands awake.
A white bird wings upriver,
    Greets the water and
Glides to silence where the
    Scars of sunset heal.

I turn to you, loins bared.
                Your hair
Floats, blonde on linen.
                The beat of darkness
Shifts the curtain.
            Your nakedness
Expects my hands which give you me,
My love, the quiver of my need.

Discovery of your body takes mine out to sea,
Past the safe harbour-bar: last
Reflections of crimson die out,
Diminishing in the glassy walls that rise,
Succeed each other, pass: and the final wave I meet
Brings oblivion, the depth of you.

I lie, cradled, heavy, midsea.
The singing in my ears falls to quiet—
Only the rustle your liquid hand
Makes on my hair.

Our skins, slowly,
Become familiar. Landfall. We alight,
Moist from the salt, and the one lamp—
Coming nearer to re-create us as a pair—
Dries us to rest.

The tide recedes.
A last wind
Touches the water as your smile lifts.
In my dark breathing you are there. The knowledge of you
Undoes a solitude called sleep.

The river holds the sleeping bird
Nightlong; a section of moon
Flicks at the water, whose profundity
Is tidal, no longer dangerous.
Lost time
Passes. The east greys. I stir
To a fresh entity. There is
A swan behind your eyelids when you wake.

HARRY GUEST

THE SNOW-LEOPARD

All day I sought it through a blaze of snow,
Elusive as the sun, its tracks a faint
Marking of claws upon the blizzard's rug.
Split off by icy curtains saw it go.

And when I trapped it, watched its spotted rage
Turn round and round the wooden ring, a dark
Journey it seemed to make in my own mind.
I felt its terror flaring in the cage.

And let it loose, retreated to the house,
Bolting those coachwood doors, those iron windows,
Hidden, afraid as its insistent cries
Turned into icicles upon the eaves.

I'd rather hear it through the crackling fire
In the neat, book-lined room, protectorate
Tight as the intellect, than hear it howling
Scratching the wooden bars in its desire,

Or whimpering for food. Rather see its breath
Make delicate shapes upon the window-glass
And hear it pounce upon the wingless birds
Than be the judge that sends it to its death.

But the brain's wisdom must be overruled:
It is my nature to consume its pride.
Next morning I shall raise my gun and go.
That leopard, my desire, cannot be fooled.

Once more I'll put it in its suffering-place,
Watch its drab paws circle a ring of dust.
I dread its pain, but suffer it I must,
And in my nightmares see no other face.

CHARLES HIGHAM

MOZART IN THETFORD

I can't enjoy music outdoors in the city,
　　For a truck goes rumbling by just
　　　　At the moment of a
　　　Delicate pianissimo,
　Or the orchestra's rise to climax is
　　　Echoed in the roar of
A plane; nor do I particularly enjoy
　　　The show of the virtuoso
　　　　Performer who
　　Arouses the crowd, whatever merits

He may have; though even he would sound better in
　　A hall with good acoustics. I
　　　　Prefer my music here,
　　　Way out in the country, where the
　Only echo is the doubled note from
　　　Across the valley. I
Like to sit on a field stone and listen to my
　　　Neighbor from half a mile away
　　　　Practice at night
　　Her reedy recorder. Or I like to

Put a record on and listen to the crimson
　　Brasses of Gabrieli roll
　　　　The hills. They might have been
　　　Meant for a high campanile
　Over a city square, but gasoline
　　　Engines have made a change
In that: so we're poorer, without some radical
　　　Change in position. Another
　　　　Piece I like to
　　Hear among the hills is the funeral

March with the long drum rolls that Purcell wrote at the
    Death of a young queen. I've never
        Heard it where one should, in
      The dark of a high cathedral;
    But sometimes, when heavy clouds have brought the
      Night in faster, and that
Clump of trees is a darker, gothic shape against
    The sky, I want another world
        To add to this:
    The roll of muffled drum beats, relieved by

Soprano voices, as clear as summer bird songs.
    But on an evening like last night,
      When the sun settles slow-
   ly down the valley, and shadows
Fall clean and sharp across a mown field, and
      Trees are like permanent
Forms on the canvases of Tuscan artists, I
    Want the quiet, assured sound of
      Four instruments
  Playing Mozart or something by Haydn.

I want the strings to replace, if only for a
    Moment, the sound of wind, not in
      Some quaint imitation,
    But with their own sound that will fill
The valley with richness and cause the deer,
      Who feed in the upper
Orchard, to pause and lift their heads high in wonder.
    I would like to think, though I know
      Better, that such
  Music was written for a place like this.

WILLIAM HOLLIS

NIGHTFALL

At nightfall, as the sea darkens,
A depth darkness thickens, mustering from the gulfs and the
    submarine badlands,
To the sea's edge. To begin with
It looks like rocks uncovering, mangling their pallor.
Gradually, the labouring of the tide
Falls back from its productions,
Its power slips back from glistening nacelles, and they are
    crabs.
Giant crabs, under flat skulls, staring inland,
Like a packed trench of helmets.
Ghosts, they are ghost-crabs.
They emerge
An invisible disgorging of the sea's cold
Over the man who strolls along the sands.
They spill inland, into the smoking purple
Of our woods and towns—a bristling surge
Of tall and staggering spectres
Gliding like shocks through water.
Our walls, our bodies, are no problem to them.
Their hungers are homing elsewhere.
We cannot see them or turn our minds from them.
Their bubbling mouths, their eyes,
In a slow mineral fury
Press through our nothingness where we sprawl on our beds,
Or sit in our rooms. Our dreams are ruffled maybe.
Or we jerk awake to the world of our possessions
With a gasp, in a sweat-burst, our brains jamming blind
Into the bulb-light. Sometimes, for minutes, a sliding
Staring
Thickness of silence
Presses between us. These crabs own this world.
All night around us, or through us,
They stalk each other, they fasten on to each other,
They mount each other, they tear each other to pieces,

They utterly exhaust each other.
They are the powers of this world.
We are their bacteria,
Dying their lives and living their deaths.
At dawn, they sidle back under the sea's edge.
They are the turmoil of history, the convulsion
In the roots of blood, in the cycles of concurrence.
To them, our cluttered countries are empty battleground.
All day they recuperate under the sea.
Their singing is like a thin sea-wind flexing in the rocks of a
    headland,
Where only crabs listen.

They are God's only toys.

TED HUGHES

AT THE DANCING SCHOOL OF
THE SISTERS SCHWARZ

Silently grave as voyeurs in a powder room
we fathers sit with coats folded on knees
this visiting day, watching Miss Hermene
teach fourteen girls the elements of ballet.

Accompaniment is struck in chords upon
the Steinway grand. Outside a siren grieves:
law for a speeder below. Miss Hermene slaps
time on her thighs, her words exact and low.

Her muscular, liquid arms demonstrate grace
to daughters in pink tights along the bar.
Battement tendu! and fourteen arches curve.
She spots a limp leg, squats for a better view,

then sweeps from child to child, chin high, commanding—
love in her old eyes, discipline on her tongue,
correct as a queen, and fierce beneath her charm.
Our girls come hushed and quick, hair back, nails clean;

chubby or bony, concave or convex of chest,
gangly, petite or tough, their slippers whisper
in the studio. No scratching or wriggling now,
but each projects life to her pointed toe.

My own, the smallest, still sticks out her tummy
curving her limber spine. Her feet are flat,
her limbs thin. Braids swing as she takes correction
like kisses—with freckly cheeks and toothy grin.

Material comes raw, but Miss Hermene
makes girlflesh pirouette and count strict time.
Covertly I squirm—loosely sitting, like nature,
thinking how daffodils look to a worm.

Glissez! Sautez! Pliez! Knees skinned at skating
now bend in diamond shapes around the room,
and fathers dream of the stage where ballerinas
are purer than people, selfless, without age.

JUDSON JEROME

THE MAN WHO INVENTED THE WHEEL

Once when the world was flat, a scandalous gnome
Being too lazy for games of weight to win
The eye of a girl with bangs and ankles and things,
Invented a wheel. Alas, I don't know how:
Still this shadowy mind, this unknown wheelwright
Somehow concerns me. Was it simply a fluke?
Was he an oaf that drunken destiny
In moments of pique assigned an errand?
Was he a man of sorrow wishing that dreams,
The vulgar kind, would visit his nights with thighs
And breasts and stratagems? Did he sit pulling
At blades of grass, amused, and watching the strong
Tussle, tossing the rocks and posing their muscles?

Did he mumble invoking the mystery
Of all inventions? Did he grumble about
Ingratitude because the tribe was lewd
With old indecent gestures making the sign
Of the frightened, echoing to the neighbors' screaming
The old derision, "Here comes you know who"?

Had he comforters with an inside track
Advising more patience toward shrill detractors,
"They're not to blame; you are ahead of your times"?
Did they suggest a leisurely trip across
The hills to learn of news in other caves?
Did he consent to reappear in spring
With tales of how the sun had burned the wheel,
Sucking the image from his addled head?

Or did he smile, knowing the dream was not
His doing; it would survive some other spring?
Then bowing politely to the council wives,
He eyed a lady with teeth and bangs and legs
And things, gave her the sign submissive, then flexed
His muscles, and went to wrestle a log or a stone.

ALLEN KANFER

BEETLE ON THE SHASTA DAYLIGHT

Hills moved. I watched their shadows
riding by like names said
only once. The oaks turned round
and leaves ran past my head.

It was all reeling back where
the old disasters hung between
locked doors stitching the air,
unheard, as if they'd never been.

And the sun came falling through
the window of the train; it filled
my lap, slid down my arms into
the aisle, a blazing river spilled

inside. I found her in the shallow
light, wearing her skeleton
strapped smooth over her belly,
wallowing on her back, alone.

Some little Pequod spitting, mastheads
tufted with joints like unfleshed frogs,
lame as a butterfly spread
on a pin. And from the thrashing legs

hooks caught at nothing, casting
and casting in the air, her
bent and beaded feelers lashing
until the threads would have to tear.

Pharaohs watched her push her dung ball
on the sand the way the sun
rolled slowly over heaven, saw
how she hatched her children

58

out of that roundness, called her Life.
They made her image out of stone,
greener than stems, to celebrate
the ornamental lake a queen

had built, to mark a lion hunt
or even marriage. They sent
her gleaming in the tombs of all
the dead so they might rise again.

I didn't touch her; slipping a marker
from my book under her back,
I turned my wrist down gently, set her
right. A piece of the whole shook

world turned up. Alive! She was
amazed to flex herself, to feel
the sun along her side like juice,
to have her front legs wheel

her forward, arched in a priestly
benediction. Oh, she was tight. She served
her concentrated self, and neatly.
Her eyes glittered out of her head.

Lightly she went and steady down
the aisle. Not any landscape she
remembered. Yet she was sure of home,
composed her dark wherever she might be

creeping. I waved her well. Saw
that she left no furrow in the floor.
But someone got up, swelling out
of his seat, and raised his foot before

my hand could drop, and put it down
and passed into the next car
and was gone. There was no sound
but the train's sound. Far

down the tracks, the sun rolled over.
I had to sit there after that
and look at California moving
backward, pressing my face flat

against the glass until it froze
to my skin. All afternoon
I looked out at the hills, those
trees with the light crawling down

their branches like white beetles
and the sky lurching among
the leaves, the shape of it tilting
at me crushed under the sun.

SHIRLEY KAUFMAN

PIERS INVENTS A NIGERIAN
NEWS-BULLETIN

"Breakfast-time: the start;
Lunch-time: the middle;
Supper-time: the end."
  Piers, aged four.

No time to go to bed, or to get up:
At supper-time the world falls over the cliff
And never knows it, presumably; at lunch
All the wide world stands level; and at breakfast:
Oh, the creation of all the days at once
In golden morning! Breakfast-time: the start!

Morning news: God created Today
Today, at seven twenty-three, with eggs,
Fanfares of bread, and jam, jubilee birds,
A conspicuous expanse of fancy sky,
And the sun, two brothers, parents, and a house,
Suddenly! from forever. Breakfast-time: the start.

Lunch-time: the middle. Bulletin: the sun
Seems to keep going up; one of the brothers
Walks and walks, and one gets angry. Sandwiches
Are an illimitable plateau. A fan
(Expected from the beginning of the world)
Evolves the wind of Paradise. Lunch, heat: the middle.

In the race of night and supper, God's night wins:
The sun goes out; the wind goes cool; dinner
Heats a few spots of table. Birds have been
Uncreated already. Invented insects
Disintegrate in shrieks. Brothers sag, worn,
And fade. Trees melt in sky. Supper: the end.

Breakfast-time; the start:
Lunch-time; the middle:
Supper-time: the end.
  Do it again, God!

DAVID KNIGHT

COUNTRY HOUSE

After a long presence of people,
after the emptying out,
the laying bare,
the walls break into conversation.
Their little hairlines ripple
and an old smile
crosses the chimney's face.

> The same flies
> endlessly drawn to the windowpanes
> hum of thirst and spiders.
> Fieldmice coast down
> a forgotten can of bacon fat.
> Two clocks tick themselves witless.
> October, clutching its blankets,
> sidles from room to room
> where the exhausted doors
> now speak to their stops,
> four scrubbed stones of common quartz.

They are gone,
those hearty moderns who came in
with their plastic cups and spoons
and restorative kits
for stripping the woodwork,
torn between making over
and making do.
At their leavetaking
the thin beds exhale.
The toilet bowl blinks,
its eye full of purple antifreeze.

As after a great drought
the earth opens its holes
to raise the water table,
the stairs undo their buttons.
The risers, each an individual,
slip out of plumb.
Seams, pores, and crazings unpucker
making ready for frost.
A tongue of water
circles the cellar wall
and locks itself in.

Soon the raccoon will come
with his four wise hands
to pick the carcass
and the salt-worshiping porcupine
will chew sweat from the porch swing.
The red squirrels will decamp,
the last litter of mice go under.
Caught and fastened, this house
will lean into the January blizzard
letting its breath go sour,
its rib cage stiffen.

MAXINE KUMIN

ARS POETICA

Severed from our deep selves, we occupy
The idle hour with music or ballet;
Under the lights the dazzled dancers play
At artful birds who die most beautifully.
Spectators, we applaud, who have preferred
The swan queen to the vivid firebird.

We are as ghosts who haunt the galleries
Until the eye bewilders. Color, line,
Poured like a blood through abstract arteries,
And the five senses drained for a clear design.
Is it the blood's detachment that dictates
These squares on squares, these greys and violets?

Faint on the parchment scrolls, our exploration
Is written with a spider's hand in gold;
Loving the curled vellums, the museum
And a bronze tablet generations scrolled,
We seek our wisdom in perpetuals,
The word of prophets, traced on stone or jewel.

And are most faithful to the artifice,
The world of form, where simulated leaves
Hang on the perfect tree in perfect space
Out of all sunlight, like our buried selves
Divided from the seasons and the sun.
We pass green country for this formal one.

JOAN LaBOMBARD

HOMO ERECTUS

A natural-born fool, if ever there was one!
But I suppose we have to give the precious half-wit his due.
Knowing absolutely nothing, understanding less,
He struggled to his feet and stood,
Knowledge or no knowledge.
But what a simpleton! An ignoramus pure and simple.
He could care less.
Standing meant absolutely nothing to him,
Except the vague pain,
The dull throb of hurt that rippled up his thighs
And twisted along his spine.
Numbskull! Really, he's almost too much.

Still, he stood; we can't deny that.
And *something* kept him up (hardly *pride*),
Kept him from giving in.
Who knows? Maybe his eyes were finally fed up
With looking down in the same old dirty rut
Day after day, time out of mind.
Damn it all, anyway,
Maybe he'd simply had enough.

One thing's for certain, though:
He stood—
You can't take that away from him,
Smile smugly as you will.
You almost have to admire him a little,
Despite his sheer stupidity.

Stupid? That's the understatement of all time!
Listen, you'll die laughing:
He actually reached up
(almost upsetting himself in the bargain)
And dumbly tried to grasp the moon and stars.
Good god, what an utter, indescribable ass!

But still, you know . . .
He stood.

WILLIAM LATTA

CAIRNS

(for Sylvia Plath)

Her death smiled from the paper,
Forewarning of distant landslides.
Something crumbles inside me, once more
The slowly established lines of communication
Are left dangling above the wreck,
The patiently built encampments in the foothills
Are blotted out, months, years wasted, a voice
Lost in the snow.
As the search is called off lethargy
Shadows the survivors like a mist.
All words are called in question, all heroic
Vigour, movement, daring, all she was . . .
Though words fail us stones shall not
And in the mist her stony words shall serve
As cairns.

The only way with death is to take it daily
In small doses with your morning paper.
Gloat over earthquakes, fires,
Tiny figures leaping from sinking liners.
Make your nerves taut, harden them to disaster.
But even then, suddenly, in bad weather,
Some virus may intrude to strike you down.
For a moment the city stalls, reels, giddily
You clutch at railings, steady yourself, smile
At the absurdity of loss; then, losing momentum,
Like the slipped carriages of an express
Trundling to a halt in a country siding,
Your world runs slowly down. Grass will in time
Stifle this bright steel. But for now, for now
There is no cure and nothing to say
That has not time and again already been said—
In vain.

The voice of a dead woman
Reads her own poems over the radio—
Presentiments, omens,
A shape on the horizon only she knew,
A burden, a growth long carried within her
Her poems now have exorcized. She lies
Still-dead. We crowd with horror
The cast of the mind we had just begun to know,
Finding how little we knew.
We the survivors are accused by her death
Of ignorance, in all our pores, of pain.
The pollarded trees brandish their crutches for pity:
We do not see.
The factory sirens scream as they disgorge
Their human fodder. We nod and pass by.
Ships in the estuary wail for the drowned:
We say, "There's a gale blowing."

Slowly eroded by successive deaths,
The forelands of my youth slip into the sea
In a whirlpool of mud, a high wave, then, settling,
The same water,
The same element that when the dam burst drowned
Thousands, yet left me dry-eyed
Though in newsreels they angled dead men out of
        the trees.
Numbers bludgeon, we ignore the one.
At the slow onset of a fatal sickness
The extremities refuse to feel pain,
Imagination's clogged, the heart wrung dry, I dread
My own impassivity.

Kind Sister Death has drawn a screen
About what was or might have been,
But we are marked and make our own
Fragments of the life that's gone.
As once the barricades are down
Looters invade the flooded town,
Among vacated flesh and blood
We leech for intellectual food.
A burning farm as we drove by
Blazoned despair through the night sky:

Distance will accommodate
The tortured cry, the loudest hate,
Wisdom, reduced to mortal pain,
Proves all the great abstractions vain.
However love clamp bone to bone
We live apart, we die alone,
Nor can mere numbers ease distress
Or make the single parting less.
Only the private grief is real
And the worst death is, not to feel.

CHRISTOPHER LEVENSON

LIFE AT WAR

The disasters numb within us
caught in the chest, rolling
in the brain like pebbles. The feeling
resembles lumps of raw dough

weighing down a child's stomach on baking day.
Or Rilke said it, "My heart . . .
Could I say of it, it overflows
with bitterness . . . but no, as though

its contents were simply balled into
formless lumps, thus
do I carry it about."
The same war

continues.
We have breathed the grits of it in, all our lives,
our lungs are pocked with it,

the mucous membrane of our dreams
coated with it, the imagination
filmed over with the gray filth of it:
the knowledge that humankind,

delicate Man, whose flesh
responds to a caress, whose eyes
are flowers that perceive the stars,

whose music excels the music of birds,
whose laughter matches the laughter of dogs,
whose understanding manifests designs
fairer than the spider's most intricate web

still turns without surprise, with mere regret
to the scheduled breaking open of breasts whose milk
runs out over the entrails of still-alive babies,
transformation of witnessing eyes to pulp-fragments,
implosion of skinned penises into carcass-gulleys.

We are the humans, men who can make;
whose language imagines *mercy, lovingkindness;*
we have believed one another
the mirrored forms of a God we felt as good—

who do these acts, who convince ourselves
it is necessary; these acts are done
to our own flesh; burned human flesh
is smelling in Viet Nam as I write.

Yes, this is the knowledge that jostles for space
in our bodies along with all we
go on knowing of joy, of love;

our nerve filaments twitch with its presence
day and night,
nothing we say has not the husky phlegm of it in
      the saying,
nothing we do has the quickness, the sureness,
the deep intelligence living at peace would have.

DENISE LEVERTOV

HANDS AND THE FISHERMAN'S WIFE

Between the halves of a dream
       I waken to his hand on my back, still
damp with seafoam and scratchy
       like fine sandpaper. Lately, he forgets
to wash. To hear him talk, you'd
       think his work was a year-long bubblebath.
Like as not, I'll find a few
       seashells or barnacles caked inside his
underthings, a strand of kelp
       looped over his ear. He drops his trousers.
Some tools clink in his pocket.
       The ring of fine steel is muffled by fish-
guts, deep tarstains, dried blood. He's
       brushing off fish-scales, two or three brittle
bone-chips, the countless layers
       of days and days overwear, so-much-kneaded
into denims, catgut
       toughened with use, they seem laminated
into the fiber of the cloth.
       Upright on the deck, of a clear day
waving good-bye, he glitters
       like fiberglass from hat to socks. And now,
this act of kindness — knowing
       I hear him scrape with his hand like a brush,
dusting the outsides to a vague-
       clean look, he angles for the smile I keep hid,
feigning sleep. How strange, to hear
       him hearing me listen, the listening
too pressed in layers and fused
       smooth with the hard wear of years. Now the
         hand
pauses with a certain pride,
       fondling stale garments that defy repeated
scrubbings on a washboard
       that sings like a whetstone on my taut arm.
The same hand passes, at length,
       to the bed-post, and I catch its odor

of bait and strewn entrails. Next,
	it falls on the inner slope of my thigh,
and settles close. The open
	palm, precise as fine lace (traces of fish-
flakes caught in the hand's creases
	like splinters), eases the flesh with a docile
roughness of loose gravel. The same
	hand that conquers the marlin after hours
of shrewd contest, gaffs whales,
	holds jaws of a blue-shark together, mans
full nets and disposes fish-
	guts with a swiftness to make breath catch—**now**
tender, releases my breath.

Laurence Lieberman

TRYING FOR SOLITUDE

If I walk on my hands
   who will follow the prints of my shoes
     on the blue beach of the sky?
Upright I am easily trailed.
I carry a gong
          (like a cow)
   round my neck.
The noise of my tongue
               as I contemplate hunger
   is enough to attract a small crowd.
I enter a room like the buzz of a fly
   and a gamut of hands seeks to slap me to death.
In the wide open air
   I am burned by the sun or the wind
     as I drag with my eyes
             every building & tree.
Someone intrudes
   thru every locked door
     I have latched for a thought.
No mind of my own,
   but a hall in a skull
     where the audience harangues
       from a thousand podiums.
If I race towards the woods
   the trees become people
     and the birds mere chattering verbs.
By the creek
   the trout
       (in a mischievous mood)
     advise me against my own will.
My guests are abundant
             bearing breezes & suns.
In the house where I dream
   there's a marathon waltz of the dead.
     A stampede of spiders & mice
       protests inside walls.

A jet in the sky
   makes tracks thru my ears.
My hounds
         (whether imagined or real)
   inflate every sound with a howl.
Behind the gloom of my face
   I am constantly guessing
     a clamor unnamed.
The wounds which silence would heal
   are incurably bruised.
The radio's trained on my head
             like a bombsight.
The cat is meowing for milk,
while the dog that is crunching a bone
   is climbing the stairs of my spine.

JACK LINDEMAN

ALREADY LATE

Already late we pull up to the house.
Shadows of the night stand in the doorway,
like Indians guarding the ritual place
of the spirits.
I pick up the child.

She is sleeping
and her body is like water.
She breathes very quietly.
She is like a brook that no one
has ever seen.

As I walk
the spirits come near,
stroking her hair and singing.
They plant four young trees
beside her shore, and in the air
they place two dragonflies
with scarlet wings
to be her companions.

An hour later when the TV goes on
I begin to weep.

Lou Lipsitz

THE DWARF

She went away from us upon a snow-white
steed, the forest virgin scented with
the rain of evergreen, to while the mythic
hours in a prince's castle. Was it right

of her to take away her apple
innocence from seven dappled
dwarfs, to arbitrarily
absent us from felicity?

She went away to share a snow-white bed
with some tall aqua velva future king
who'll never know the pleasure wrested
from a woman willing yet unwilling,

nor how bigly bad a simple tree
appears to a tiny man, nor will they ever
either of them know the human thing
is not to be snow-white but to be ugly.

GERALD LOCKLIN

THE SHELL

Since the shell came and took you in its arms
   Whose body was fine bone
That walked in light beside a place of flowers,
    Why should your son
Years after the eclipse of those alarms
   Perplex this bitten stone
For some spent issue of the sea? Not one
Blue drop of drying blood I could call ours

In all that ocean that you were remains
   To move again. I come
Through darkness from a distance to your tomb
    And feel the swell
Where a dark flood goes headlong to the drains.
   I hear black hailstones drum
Like cold slugs on your skin. There is no bell
To tell what drowned king founders. Violets bloom

Where someone died. I dream that overhead
   I hear a bomber drone
And feel again stiff pumping of slow guns
    Then the All Clear's
Voice break, and the long summing of the dead
   Below the siren's moan
Subdue the salt flood of all blood and tears
To a prolonged strained weeping sound that stuns.

I turn in anger. By whatever stars
   Clear out of drifting rack
This winter evening I revive my claim
    To what has gone
Beyond your dying fall. Through these cold bars
   I feel your breaking back
And live again your body falling on
That flood of stone where no white Saviour came

On Christian feet to lift you to the verge
   Or swans with wings of fire
Whose necks were arched in mourning. Black as coal
    I turn to go
Out of the graveyard. Headstone shadows merge
   And blur. I see the spire
Lift over corpses. And I sense the flow
Of death like honey to make all things whole.

GEORGE MACBETH

INCIDENT

I am going to tell you what happened.
The dog is in it, the blindman,
the butcher picking his teeth with a match,
and a street skinny with afternoon.
Not that you asked to hear, and, maybe,
won't want to, but you've been circling the crowd,
pirouetting on your toes as if you did.

What's difficult is how to start.
With the dog? the blindman? the match
scraping the molars of the butcher?
Begin with the afternoon that began with the morning.
Or begin with the moment you arrived at the scene,
heard rumors, wondered just what you were doing
when it happened: scratching your thigh,
shifting unpleasant thoughts in your mind
like seasons in the hands of a god;
for it is about you, this story, in the end:
it is to you the dog is dead, who tugged
the blindman seven years along this street—
the same blindman crouching in the doorway now,
his hands white, the fingers smooth,
fragrant with shadow and empty of sight
with the loss of the dog.

The butcher standing near the cop
propels the match about his dentures
with his tongue, admits he cleaved the dog in two
because he hated it and had to kill.
Possibly he saw it as a side of beef
which somehow got away; and for seven years
it haunted him, a dream that passed his shop each day,
guiding, helping the one he really had despised,
the blindman, who didn't even know he chopped,
sweated, watched him through the window of his shop.
Maybe he'd seen the blindman's hands one day,
so smoothly cool, unlike his own,
which bore the teeth marks of the cleaver and the knife.
Or tired of snapping matches with his teeth,
he may have simply wanted anyone
to populate the ice box of his day.

Shadows lengthen, and you can tell
the afternoon is tilting on toward evening.
The dog is dead beneath the sheet;
blood tightens on the sidewalk where he lies.
The blindman wears his hands like gloves along his legs,
squats silent in the doorway,
looking at the pavement he can't see,
and maybe listens to the butcher,
who grins, talking with the cop.

Well, that's the story, all I know of it.
You can forget it now, or bring it home
wrapped carefully in your interest
to open fold by fold in the dark quiet
of the apartment. Fold by fold on the table,
until a loose jelly emerges from the wrapping
and glows in the dark. Sit watching it.
Poke it. Smack it. Squeeze it, its green light
defining the black interior of your room.
This is the light the blindman sees by,
touching his way toward home;

the light the dog watched shaking in bones,
in water, in the blindman's fingers on his snout,
the light that finally cleaved him to his death.
This light the butcher lived with seven years,
and lives with now, spreading paper on the meat,
switching the light off in his shop.
This, the light of an afternoon
fallen beyond the buildings and their lives.

And us? We have only the story between us,
speech, the movement of hands. We say goodnight,
separate, walk narrowing streets,
who have become each other's story
in a tale told by another
somewhere beyond this street. The dog
is in it, the blindman, the butcher,
and the speech of two men winding
like luminous taffy in the dark:
a soft thing, a departing light,
a presence they shape with their going
and bear beneath their overcoats
like hidden burdens, although they carry it
more like children than contraband.

MORTON MARCUS

SATYR

See him in sequestered shade,
White-panted, clear-eyed, handing round the cakes.
He play acts, offers the forms,
Convincingly at ease, almost.

He sits beside you. The whites of his eyes
Are clear porcelain. He smells
Of fresh cotton. From the chair arm
His hand dangles, perfectly manicured.

Something he does not speak about, declare.
Even if you pry. He is tamed too well.
He has learned too well his lessons
In the sun.

You cannot see him later growing taut
And muscled in his private room,
Watching a forest growing round his feet,
Hearing the distant bark of wild beasts.

You cannot see him part a foliage
Wet with summer perfume, nor see him touch
Warm moonlight, palpable as flesh.
You cannot hear his tight growl of anguish

Nor know the sudden itch of thick, short hair.
You cannot see the horns thrust out,
Claws breaking his calloused skin,
His hard hooves, goatshape, pawing the figured rug.

R. D. Mathews

GOD WILL BE A LITTLE LATE THIS YEAR

THIS STABLE BEING OCCUPIED, BY TROOPS OF THIS OR THAT PER-
SUASION, AND THE CRIB BEING REQUISITIONED AS A STORAGE-BIN
FOR GEAR OF UNKNOWN MANUFACTURE, LIBERTY TO STOP BY THIS
CONVENIENT INN IS STRINGENTLY CURTAILED; ALL GROUPS, EX-
CEPT OF DULY-NOTED PERSONNEL, ARE SUSPECT, AND ARE APT TO
BE ATTACKED; NO FACTS MAY BE REVEALED OF OUR EXACT LOCA-
TION, BUT WE ARE NOT FAR FROM HELL.

———

yet history, even here, assumes in part
the classic stance: here baffled wisemen seek,
and poor men guard their fields, and herods speak
in varied accents and unvarying tones;
the cities gulp the frantic and afraid;
the hills and valleys choke themselves on bones;
here man has reached an end, and who shall start
love's penetration of hate's barricade?

———

rejected, cornered, outcast, born in strife . . .
what Child is this who crashes through to life?

J. H. McCANDLESS

A RESURRECTION

A quick-lime phoenix, so to death
For death's solution I now go.
The mildewed pyre receives my rest,
Its flames as grey as thawing snow.

It is such heavy fire that gives
Death after death, and so I rise,
A bird with ashy feather-tips,
Alive again to compromise.

And beauty dwelt with kindness once
And once the sky was tall, they say.
My flight lets fall a little dust.
My wings are on their mortal way.

RAEBURN MILLER

THE TROUT

For Barrie Cooke

Flat on the bank I parted
Rushes to ease my hands
In the water without a ripple
And tilt them slowly downstream
To where he lay, light as a leaf,
In his fluid sensual dream.

Bodiless lord of creation
I hung briefly above him
Savoring my own absence
Senses expanding in the slow
Motion, the photographic calm
That grows before action.

As the curve of my hands
Swung under his body
He surged, with visible pleasure.
I was so preternaturally close
I could count every stipple
But still cast no shadow, until

The two palms crossed in a cage
Under the lightly pulsing gills.
Then (entering my own enlarged
Shape, which rode on the water)
I gripped. To this day I can
Taste his terror on my hands.

JOHN MONTAGUE

86

DARK AND DARK

Slowly now, and softly now, and sweetly
The earth in its spin carries us into communion
With the big darkness set with its dancing stars.
The small lights of the small, nearby darkness
Come on, house lamps and street lamps. But trees and hedges
Block and confuse them. My yard, like the rolling sky,
Has just enough light to say that darkness is there.

I think of the nested thrasher out in the fence,
Closely enfolding her eggs in the grassy weaving
Established between wire mesh and the thrusting limbs
Of the old wild grape that scrambles and sprawls so broadly
That it takes from the fence its nature of thin uprightness,
And makes it suggest, in the dark, some primitive long-house,
Or perhaps an extended burial mound. I wonder

Whether the darkness enfolding the bird's awareness
Is the big darkness that dwarfs the innumerable stars,
Or only the little darkness of the fussy crust
Of earth, that is always fretting to increase the number
Of its little lights, as though it could thus deny
What lies all around it. I think that a being of the wild
Must retain the wild in its heart, however surrounded

By all the pretensions of tameness. It feels the big dark.
Grape leaves are broad; the beams of the small lights strike
    them
Like weak, stray arrows that glance from impervious shields.
The trunk of a hackberry rises as broad as a hill
To shelter a bird from everything lying behind it.
   The dark that contains the stars, and renders them tiny,
Contains too the bird, softly and sweetly enfolds her.

W. R. Moses

SCARECROW

Honeysuckle grows over the sleeve
Inside out. Once used as a scarecrow
A canvas jacket splashed with red paint
Thrown over a fence,
Keeps the shape of someone's body; despite
Summer that burned the field brown by mid-August,
Winter that froze an oak tree's knuckle,
Despite grubs, the mildew, the six inch nails.

I should be grateful if my poems
Keep some shape, out in the open field,
Year after year, a thing like this canvas
Splashed with mock blood, scaring off nothing.
The harvest is in.
Now the field snail lodges in my cuff:
I wink at the sky, all weathers, all creatures,
Telling them to come on.

STANLEY MOSS

THE MARRIAGE OF HEAVEN AND EARTH

Firelight in sunlight, silver-pale
Streaming with emerald, copper, sapphire
Ribbons and rivers, banners, fountains—
They rise, they run swiftly away.

Now apple logs unlock their sunlight
In the many-windowed room to meet
New sunlight falling in silvered gold
Through the fern-ice forest of the glass
Whose tropic surface light may pierce
But not the eye. O, early world,
Still Daphne of the stubborn wood
Singing Apollo's song in light;
O, pulsing constancies of flame
Warping a form along the log's
Slowly disintegrating face,
Crackled and etched, so quickly aged—
These are my mysteries to see
And say and celebrate with words
In orders until now reserved.

For light is in the language now,
Carbon and sullen diamond break
Out of the glossary of earth
In holy signs and scintillations,
Release their fiery emblems to
Renewal's room and morning's room
Where sun and fire once again
Phase in the figure of the dance
From far beginnings here returned,
Leapt from the maze at the forest's heart,
O, moment where the lost is found!

HOWARD NEMEROV

I, ICARUS

There was a time when I could fly. I swear it.
Perhaps, if I think hard for a moment, I can even tell you the
  year.
My room was on the ground floor at the rear of the house.
My bed faced a window.
Night after night I lay on my bed and willed myself to fly.
It was hard work, I can tell you.
Sometimes I lay perfectly still for an hour before I felt my
  body rising from the bed.
I rose slowly, slowly, until I floated three or four feet above
  the floor.
Then, with a kind of swimming motion, I propelled myself
  toward the window.

Outside, I rose higher and higher, above the pasture fence,
  above the clothesline, above the dark, haunted trees
  beyond the pasture.
And, all the time, I heard the music of the flutes.
It seemed the wind made this music.
And sometimes there were voices singing.
All of this was a long time ago and I cannot remember the
  words the voices sang,
but I know I flew when I heard them.

ALDEN NOWLAN

A CASTLE ON THE DANUBE

Surely truth is the universe of the very young;
Surely it belonged to us, a household of children
With so much time.
Or if I am wrong, consider those who sit
On lawns or in bedrooms assembling
The blue myth of childhood, the splendid
Passage of years combining to such leisure.
For three years before my grandmother died she sat
Imperial on the dark porch of summer
Recalling her life in a castle that bordered the Danube,—
Who was two years old when she rode in her father's arms
To the edge of Ohio.

           Say the old,
"I remember, I remember," but surely it is not anymore
The truth they offer. For what, from those narrow files,
Would draw small listeners from the sun? Grandmother,
It was no harm, I think,
The way you called to us and when we were gathered
Like a last fragile blessing,
Rowed us to that blue river,
Borrowed in your need another kingdom, and drew us
One by one through the mad castle door.

                          MARY OLIVER

THE BURIAL OF THE ASHES

I

I take you from the church,
in a brown leathery
cube. I cannot read
the label, the facts
of ash. A car, passing,
throws sun against
my face—a clarion.

I ask for a shovel.
"No trouble," says the
preacher. I follow,
walking lightly, my
feet seem winged,
pass through
Gethsemane.

We have trouble
with the shovel:
gone from its place—
a plain fact askew.

I fear that the winds
will howl soundless
again.

We find a spade,
though not the one
we wished, and I
lead the way
to a bush on a
rolling slope
wet with rock
like the fringe
of a well.
The crown of the
green bush wavers.

I open the box:
a sack, translucent,
crammed with scraps
of brown black white
and yellow bone.
I test the weight,
press the sack to my
cheek, hold it
to my eyes.

Sun streams through,
turns that ivory to
gold, that pale pale
white to blue, those bits
of brown to red!

II

I break the earth
(the spade moves well).
I prune a root
and smooth the hole.
I press the earth
by hand, drop in
a leaf, harbinger,
and kneel.
I crumble-in loam.
The grains slip easily!
I hunger to count them,
I hunger to count them.

I hope for silence,
vision, a shimmering
saint with golden feet
bearing a twig
studded with emeralds,
a gift.

Richard, Richard,
there was snow that day
and sun enough
to dazzle empires
when you ran laughing
beside the frosty lake,
mortal, lovely, mine.

ROBERT PETERS

NO IDENTITY

Against the name of the place we mean to move to
The guidebook bleakly rules *No identity*:
What Doctor Pevsner means is absence of ancient
Or markworthy buildings.
                                    What he implies
Is a shallowly-rooted community, a huddlement
Of not very settled commuters, interspersed with retired
Couples, tending to dwindle to widows,
Little communal sense or parish pride,
And the usual private or commonplace fears
Like that of being moved to some distant branch
Of one's place of work, or of cold old age.

But if a triumphal arch were to welcome us
What better inscription than this, *No identity*?
We are not the sort who wish to reflect prestige
From a rare environment. By possessing antique
Or using the newest things we feel no need
To reinforce our own identity; at our age
That seems unambiguous enough.
                                    My need
As a poet (not every poet's) is this—
To be immersed in a neutral solution, which
Alone provides an interim, until through the grey
Expectant film invisible writing comes clean.

No identity can be a desirable thing:
To have a face with features noticed less
Than one's range of expression, so that photographed
It never looks twice the same, and people say
"But that's not you!"

One would like to reply:
"No, that's not me, because I'm incapable
Of starting the very least personality cult.
I have freed myself at last from being me;
Don't think of me as chameleon or actor; if I take
Protective colouring, it is that I mean to be
A kind of medium, free to enjoy, well, *no identity*."

WILLIAM PLOMER

THE HAUNTED ARMCHAIR

"and hid his lord's money." (Matthew 25)

I want it not to go wrong. I want nothing to go wrong.
I shall guard and hedge and clip to the end of my days
So that nothing goes wrong. This body, this perfect body
That came from my mother's womb undiseased, wholesome,
No, nothing must go wrong. It is not I. It is not I.
No, it is not I. I is lodged in its head's centre,
Its turret, a little towards its eyes; it is not I, it is not I
        but it is mine
And an over-ranking shame to disease it, to let it disease.
I wash my hands, I wash my hands, I wash my hands once,
        twice, thrice,
I rinse my eyes with the sterile saline; I close, I pull the thick
        curtain,
I close the door and lock it, once, twice, thrice, I sit, I lie,
        I sleep in the great armchair,
And I sleep. Sleep, sleep is the preservative, cultivate sleep,
        it keeps me perfect.
No, no, it is not I; I lives only in the turret;
It is the body, it is the body, it is the body is the loved thing,
It is from my mother, it is my mother's,
It came from my mother, it is an organ of the body of my
        mother
And I shall keep it with no rough touch upon it
No rough disease to ramp up and down in it. The world?
And the world? That is the mind's. In the turret. And now
        I will sleep.
I will sleep now, for my body exists. That is enough.
Something wakes me. Is it the fire?
It crackles like a speech. The buffet of winds, the cracks
Of the beams, the taste of the sun, the swimming shark of
        the moon?
No, I think, no, I think, I think I hear time flowing,
No, I think I hear time eroding, the cinder withering in the
        grate,
The grate withering with the time, my hands raised to my
        eyes
Where my eyes are withering, I look close at my
        withering hands. How long?

How much time have I seen withering? Did I come here
    today?
Suddenly everything grants me withering. Shall I sit here
    again?
The body is gone. I sit here alone. A nothing, a virgin
    memory.
A grease-spot. A dirty chair-back.

PETER REDGROVE

HAPAX,

Or, The Same Poem Over and Over

Holy Week. Once more the full moon
Blooms in deep heaven
Like a crystal flower of ice.
The wide winter constellations
Set in fog brimming over
The seaward hills. Out beyond them,
In the endless dark, uncounted
Minute clots of light go by,
Billions of light years away,
Billions of universes,
Full of stars and their planets
With creatures on them swarming
Like all the living cells on the earth.
They have a number, and I hold
Their being and their number
In one suety speck of jelly
Inside my skull. I have seen them
Swimming in the midst of rushing
Infinite space, through a lens of glass
Through a lens of flesh, on a cup of nerves.
The question is not
Does being have meaning,
But does meaning have being.
What is happening?
All day I walk over ridges
And beside cascades and pools
Deep into the Spring hills.
Mushrooms come up in the same spot
In the abandoned clearing.
Trillium and adder's tongue
Are in place by the waterfall.
A heron lifts from a pool
As I come near, as it has done
For forty years, and flies off
Through the same gap in the trees.
The same rush and lift of flapping wings,
The same cry, how many
Generations of herons?

The same red tailed hawks court each other
High on the same rising air
Above a grassy steep. Squirrels leap
In the same oaks. Back at my cabin
In the twilight an owl on the same
Limb moans in his ancient language.
Billions and billions of worlds
Full of beings larger than dinosaurs
And smaller than viruses, each
In its place, the ecology
Of infinity.
I look at the rising Easter moon
The flowering madrone gleams in the moonlight
The bees in the cabin wall
Are awake. The night is full
Of flowers and perfume and honey.
I can see the bees in the moonlight
Flying to the hole under the window,
Glowing faintly like the flying universes.
What does it mean. This is not a question, but
    an exclamation.

KENNETH REXROTH

ABERFAN: UNDER THE ARC LIGHTS

Ask what was normal in green nature and its pain:
Will rain undermine our homes and us again?
Ask those scrabbling garden-breakers, the mountain sheep
Where are the classroom's children?—and then weep.

O martyred town shorn of its crown of glory!
That dumpy matriarch scanning in our fury
For faces of first-borns in the two handed-bier;
All the elements of tragedy are here.

Waters of history still in midnight's deep
Drip in Ceridwen's cauldrons; rage eisteddfod, seep
Into the jagged stalactites of hearts' hours.
Crushed out of life like paper-petalled flowers.

Ask courting couples whose coats took dust off the tips;
And hand back to the heavens stars on the future lips;
Children conceived in mist whose playground it had made.
Blame breeds guilt with blind anger in its road.

The whole bare drama played out as it looms
To a world-shared audience in their evening room;
One human chain of rescue under arc-light glare.
All the elements of tragedy are here.

KEIDRYCH RHYS

THE KNOT

In the heart of the queen anne's lace, a knot of blood.
For thirty years I never saw it.

Thirty years of metallic vision,
spears glancing off a bright eyeball,

suns off a Swiss lake.
A foaming meadow, the Milky Way,

and all those years the tiny dark-red spider
sitting in the whiteness of the bridal web,

waiting to plunge his crimson knifepoint
into the white apparencies.

Little wonder the eye, healing, sees
for a long time through a mist of blood.

ADRIENNE RICH

PAIN FOR A DAUGHTER

Blind with love, my daughter
has cried nightly for horses,
those long-necked marchers and churners
that she has mastered, any and all,
reining them in like a circus hand—
the excitable muscles and the ripe neck—
tending, this summer, a pony and a foal.
She who is too squeamish to pull
a thorn from the dog's paw
watched her pony blossom with distemper,
the underside of the jaw swelling
like an enormous grape.
Gritting her teeth with love,
she drained the boil and scoured it
with hydrogen peroxide until pus
ran like milk on the barn floor.

Blind with loss all winter,
in dungarees, a ski jacket, and a hard hat,
she visits the neighbors' stable,
our acreage not zoned for barns,
they who own the flaming horses
and the swan-whipped thoroughbred
that she tugs at and cajoles,
thinking it will burn like a furnace
under her small-hipped English seat.

Blind with pain, she limps home.
The thoroughbred has stood on her foot.
He rested there like a building.
He grew into her foot until they were one.
The marks of the horseshoe printed
into her flesh, the tips of her toes
ripped off like pieces of leather,
three toenails swirled like shells
and left to float in blood in her riding boot.

Blind with fear, she sits on the toilet,
her foot balanced over the washbasin,
her father, hydrogen peroxide in hand,
performing the rites of the cleansing.
She bites on a towel, sucked in breath,
sucked in and arched against the pain,
her eyes glancing off me where
I stand at the door, eyes locked
on the ceiling, eyes of a stranger,
and then she cries . . .
Oh, my God, help me!
Where a child would have cried *Mama!*
Where a child would have believed *Mama!*
She bit the towel and called on God,
and I saw her life stretch out . . .
I saw her torn in childbirth,
and I saw her, at that moment,
in her own death, and I knew that she
knew.

ANNE SEXTON

YOUR FACE ON THE DOG'S NECK

It is early afternoon.
You sit on the grass
with your rough face on the dog's neck.
Right now
you are both as still as a snapshot.
That infectious dog ought to let a fly bother her,
ought to run out in an immense field,
chasing rabbits and skunks,
mauling the cats, licking insects off her rump,
and stop using you up.
My darling, why do you lean on her so?
I would touch you—
that pulse brooding under your madras shirt,
each shoulder the most well-built house,
the arms, thin birches that do not escape the breeze,
the white teeth that have known me,
that wait at the bottom of the brook,
and the tongue, my little fish! . . .
But you are stopped in time.

So I will speak of your eyes,
although they are closed.
Tell me, where is each stubborn-colored iris?
Where are the quick pupils that make
the floor tilt under me?
I see only the lids, as tough as riding boots.
Why have your eyes gone into their own room?
Good night they are saying
from their little leathery doors.
Or shall I sing of eyes
that have been ruined with mercy and lust,
and once with your own death,
when you lay bubbling like a caught fish,
sucking on the manufactured oxygen?

Or shall I sing of eyes
that are resting so near the hair
of that hateful animal?
Love twists me, a Spanish flute plays in my blood,
and yet I can see only
your little sleep, an empty place.

But when your eyes open
against the wool stink of her thick hair,
against the faint sickening neck of that dog,
whom I envy like a thief,
what will I ask?
Will I speak up, saying
there is a hurried song, a certain seizure
from which I gasp?
Or will your eyes lie in wait,
little field mice nestling on their paws?
Perhaps they will say nothing,
perhaps they will be dark and leaden,
having played their own game
somewhere else,
somewhere far off.

Oh, I have learned them, and know that
when they open and glance at me
I will turn like a little dancer,
and then, quite simply,
and all by myself,
I will fall,
bound to some mother/father,
bound to your sight,
bound for nowhere
and everywhere.

Or perhaps, my darling,
because it is early afternoon,
I will forget that my voice is full of good people,
forget how my legs could sprawl on the terrace,
forget all that the birds might witness—
the torn dress, the shoes lost in the arbor—
while the neighbor's lawnmower bites and spits out
some new little rows of innocent grass.
Certainly,
I need not speak of it at all.
I will crouch down
and put my cheek near you,
accepting this spayed and flatulent bitch you hold,
letting my face rest in an assembled tenderness
on the old dog's neck.

ANNE SEXTON

IMPERFECT SYMPATHIES

Kit Carson might be surprised
To see his grave stone with its edges chipped
Fluted, by relic seekers, to a blade.
He might be gratified that so many wished
Something to prove they had been near his bones
And found his country of long-leaved cottonwoods
Making a fragile shade against a sky
Immoderately blue, the adobe walls
Buttressed by purple shadow, the little voice
Of the irrigation ditch that spoke of mountains.

But he might feel a lack of fellowship
With these late comers. Only a century
Set him apart from them, but his had been
A less alleviated life which left
One little opportunity to ponder
What were man's greatest goods:
The cold, the thirst, the hunger making the answer,
The fire behind the windbreak, the scanty seep
In the bottom of the arroyo, the rabbit carcass.
It probably never occurred to him to question
The reason for suffering or man's existence.
Without antidote or anesthetic
The hand bitten by the rattler, or the leg
Crushed by the falling horse engrossed the thought.
And why one lived was not a primary concern
With the trail steep, the darkness deepening, the snow falling.

CLARICE SHORT

FLATFISH

It moves vertically through salted
Pressures, with a head that sees sideways.
The nets are submerged, which it enters.
Nothing to come for specially. Men want it.

The white flesh powered by a tail filmed with skin
Sways its mild hulk into their fold.
The white flesh is food. When boiled,
It flakes easily off the bone.

Is this love? God created us
For the toothed shark, the molestation
Of two jaws hinged through flesh
Onto each other's hooked teeth.

Its ethics are formal, determined.
Otherwise He made the mild flatfish,
And gleaning mackerel that fatten
On the dead's helplessness strengthening its rancid colours.

He made the flatfish, their eyes
Naïve as a bead drawn from a leopard's skin.
Their white flesh is flaked into the mossy,
Acidic belly, just hanging.

The good salt, phosphate, each dissolved
Into flesh. The fish are left to gasp
In ships' holds, mulcting the air
For air moving in the gill's membrane

Miserly, useless. A gradual pain
Until the fish weaken. Could they cry
We might gas them to concert
Their distress. Nets are men's media,

Their formal, knotted, rectangular intelligence.
They survive on what the fish weighs, their welfare
Accurate as a pair of scales.

We are not going to change.
But husband the sea, planting the fish spawn in
    The frigid heft of plot-water
      Grey, but not stone.

    Mackerel will gorge
A sea parsley, its flowers sprinkled with white, granular petal;
    The shark will eat mud
      At the sea's foundation.

    Though to reap will be by net,
As many fish as grains husked from their flattened case,
    The ear raped of its oval bolus
      Folded into itself.

    The precise allotment of fish
A growth in kind; pollination by a brush tasked
    Onto differing species
      For the flesh's good.

    The flesh's good. Elsewhere
We seized on our own kind, not for food. Each fish
    Glides through a forest,
      An oily lung

    Of sea weed, the swell
Moved in a land-grafted integument of sea plant. A uniform
    Thicket moon-masted, its foliage
      Begins to lock

    Fast with sea-forester's
Skill. We evolve with our hands and brain. The pad of each
    Hand, moist; the nails sharp
      As a grown fin.

                                      JON SILKIN

CHILDREN

Children hardier than we think
run from the exile of their hurt,
become as public as a park;

or bundled in love from the sick room
of roses break, escape those fans
of fears waving in love's looks,
naked shoot the lake of swans;

quick to forge a link,
lose separateness in companies of the grass,
stream in light at times through others
who contain them like a glass;

in a summer of their own
swim the foam of leaves,
float on tide's gold-green
winged in weather-welcoming skin;

live the lore of their kind
in the gas-house yard of heroes,
under the sun's banners shine,
mounting in fame like golden dollars.

And when the voyage ends,
under the lintel of home pride bends,
where disguised in open looks
they lock themselves in their own legends.

KAY SMITH

THE LOON'S NECKLACE

I

Gavia immer, it says, and reminds me of a prissy appelation,
   A bookish monicker, or a baptismal name;
And maybe if you hadn't been a bird you might have been a
                        scholar
   Or a priest, for everybody snickers at your pitiful pre-
                       occupation
With poetry and paradise. There's no use hiding that you're
                       lame
   On earth — everyone knows an easy touch, a sucker for a
                       holler
From a hunter, a bloody nuisance in the fisherman's seine.

II

Fish-snapper too. Watching the slide of spring migration,
   You're not above a passionate peck at a fin or an eye.
Ataata[1] Mmarik thought you worse than seaweed, cluttering
                       up his net
   In your disconcerting willingness to die,
When he fished you out of the water, ludicrous and wet,
   Nothing but skin and bone, and a miserable consolation
To the fish he threw you to, though multiplied for whatever
                       hungry set.

III

Miracle still you are, though "crazy as a loon"'s an affectation
   Which I conjecture came from the days of Anglo-Saxon rune
When a happy *haeleth* wandering home at night
   From the mead-hall, head full of beer and the harper's tune,
Thought he saw a pointed peak on a broom with floppy-
                       footed flight,

[1] Father.

Thought he heard a witch's cackling malediction,
But it was you — flapping your slow iambic wings across the
orange moon.

IV

Whether miracle or myth, I have no reservation
    About the nature of your touchy soul.
The raven could hardly guess, when he gave that extra stick
    Of the needle dipped in the train-oil bowl,
As he worked around the circlet on your neck,
    That you'd fly off the handle in frivolous irritation
All because of one accidental little prick,

V

And fling the bowl at him and make him black;
    Nor, stalking out in stiff-necked indignation,
Did it dawn on you that he would fling it back
    And hit your legs and leave you crippled for eternity,
So that, loon-lonely, you were forced to get the knack
    Of taking off from water to reach your airy aspiration
Or of plumbing for the silvery muses in the sea.

VI

But they were ruthless! — skinning you alive
    And yanking out your feathers — O! the scorpion grins! —
As they tossed you in the air — filthy destructive hate and
no compassion! —
    Making a scapegoat of you for their own inhuman sins —
And still go on! But God, wishing his own to thrive,
    Rescued you from their roughness, soothed your passion,
And left the taunters open-mouthed to save their skins

VII

As best they could, through the long winter season,
    Snowing from winter, snowing from spring to fall.
Of course, there was no summer and there were no seals,

No life upon the sea. Those who survived were lucky to
                                   survive at all,
Those haughty hunters hungry, reduced to dogs and boots
                                   and heels,
    And dying off — except, and with sufficient reason,
The ingenious ones who hacked the bodies and turned
                                   cannibal.

VIII

But life goes on — and with it the returning spring,
    The sunny sky, earth's cleansing inundation
Of melting snows and streams, and the far wavering cry
    Of the returning loon, circling on the wing,
Hovering near the haunts of men with heaven's benediction.
    Well, that's the story — but I would be a fool to try
To say what myth is, or reality, or any blessed thing.

IX

And what about that silly ornament around your neck?
    Shall we believe it has some deep signification,
A solemn symbol of a spirit serving God?
    An inescapable reminder of your daily obligation
To count the oily beadings as you preen and peck
    Your feathers, a figuration of the bloody path He trod?
Shall we laugh? This clown! who with a cackle only answers
                                   back.

X

Or shall we rage! Only a useless scarecrow of a kite,
    Crazy at that, unsavory to the fork and knife,
And suffering's not within our modern dispensation:
    Just television murder, intellectual pride, sophisticated shite!
We want no skin-pricked way! No way to life!
    No *via dolorosa* sign to ruin our vacation
At the lake, where we can quarrel with the children and the
                                   wife!

XI

Where does the priest begin, the poet find his termination?
   There is no ending, foolish fish! For there's the hunter too,
The woman at the fire, the scholar, and the child.
   We're all a part of nature fading into richer shades of blue,
And the sun, flooding the sky with her sisterly imagination,
   Will find us in the morning, though the night was terrible
                     and wild,
Rising in the quickening grasses, glittering with dew,

XII

By the lake grasses which murmur of incomprehensible things,
   Of spring's spawning, of avian exultation,
Of the loon's return with love and God's plasticities.
   O spirit-bird! Sprinkle me with your *aspergillum* wings,
Fluff and feather our insane inflexibilities
   That we, land-ugly, can become lake-beautiful,
Can lurch into the air and cry for joy at our transfiguration,
   No longer awkward flying, love-obedient and death-
                     dutiful.

ALEX. SPALDING

THE LATE VISITOR

Listen, let me explain, it was not the fire
That burned in the hearth and kept me there.
It was no real fire, though I swear it did seem so
And to go out was to step into blackest snow,
And to stay was to lose, not find. Words only say
What is gone. Or are motions like flame and snow,
Slow circlings of something about to occur,
The birth of a salamander in the fire.

I am caught between never and now. You must tell me to go.

ANN STANFORD

LETTER FROM A FRIEND IN EXILE

. . . I move among them, neither spy nor slave,
though like a spy I hoard my poverty
and like a slave I count their property
as something strange, and good, and not my own—
for what I touch here, brick, or bark, or bone,
does not touch back the way my fingers felt
the gritty answer of my crumbling hearth
the day I threw my name upon the fire
and ran my nail across the mantel's crack;
(it wandered, like a river on a map).

But that map's gone, and my lost country gone,
names of cities changed, our temples toppled.
Our children have been herded into pens,
our strong men run away to rocks and caves,
our women tossed like baggage on the shields
of the barbarian. And I am here, in exile,
ghost of a guest to all the gentle hosts.

Ingratitude? No. Thanks are in my heart:
I thank these men for the sound their footsteps make
in the safe night, for their moon's long-legged strut,
their silver Daddy puffing on his pipe
in fifty miles of corn. I thank the dawn
for happening in the sure way it does,
like a fine woman, with her apron gathered,
draping the light's clean clothes on all the lines.
I thank them when I close the door on them,
and hear their voices laughing down the hall,
then fading, as though voices became birds,
and fussed upon the branches, and grew still.
Like eager mutes, the shadows talk to me,
and in the darkness all my shades agree.

But what man needs a friend who cannot grieve
when it is time for him to grieve, a friend
who puts his war too soon away from him?
If home is where the heart is, as you say,
then I still burn for my own broken hearth.
You must forgive this, as the sun forgives
the balked raid of the night on your bright fields.

FELIX STEFANILE

WAITING

Ulysses waiting
Inside that equine wooden egg,
Cramped in a foetal posture
Breathing the foetid air,
Hearing the light laughter of women
Wafted on the perfumed breeze
Of the wide-wombed Trojan night;

And Jonah, that other insider,
He too saw the view from the belly of the beast—
Uniform, all-enclosing, desolate,
As though a flower should close into a bud
And the bud shrink into a seed
And the seed go back into its socket
And the branch droop and drop off
Blackened, withered, utterly useless!

And Joseph pitifully bound for Egypt,
And Daniel, Shadrach, Meshach, Abednego,
And you, Lord Jesus, hidden in a cave
Like crocuses and daffodils under the frozen ground;

I applaud your cunning inertia,
The gathering of strength preceding your final birth.

WARREN STEVENSON

TREE SERVICE

Jockey, juggler, rider of ropes and leaves,
climber with metal thorns nailed to his feet,
he kicks dust back, stomps upward on his spurs
until his yellow bump hat bobs and gleams
among the antlers of a dying beast.

I could not save it, and it hung too near,
with blackening horns aimed for the house,
but I am bothered by this hired shape
going up through the dead lace of boughs
that never felt a sharper tooth than sleet.

Yet I must back him, since his life is pitched
against an overgrown and staglike head
assembling ruin above my roof,
though dreading the first severed branch
and its steep plunge.
                      It falls, scattering rot
like chaff from a broken star; more sky moves in.
I miss the reaching claw. A hoof goes next—
it paced for years above my fires and mist—
and I perceive how easily space grows
around a saw.
              He swings and sears,
agile as a toy, the round hat floating
like a crown. I feel an office worker's awe
of his hard, bustling thighs and arms.

Only the rough, round trunk remains.
A portion falls, the sound heart glowing red
against a litter of gray, scattered veins,
witness to how communication failed
between the blowing top and the dark nerves
that worked in ignorance to feed a dying crest.

The saw is still at last, and still the great stump
throbs and shines, the hidden taproot busy as before,
cell, core, and tissue storing useless fat.
The sky looks bare. The wind is high and keen;
it draws a knife against my back.
I am aware of other branches, blades,
and the saw's dust, like a bright cap,
covering my cold and brittle hair.

ADRIEN STOUTENBURG

CAUSES

"Questioned about why she had beaten her spastic child to death,
the mother told police, 'I hit him because he kept falling off
his crutches.' "—News item.

Because one's husband is different from one's self,
the pilot's last words were "Help, my God, I'm shot!"
Because the tip growth on a pine looks like Christmas tree
    candles,
cracks appear in the plaster of old houses.

And because the man next door likes to play golf,
a war started up in some country where it is hot,
and whenever a maid waits at the bus-stop with her
    bundles,
the fear of death comes over us in vacant places.

It is all foreseen in the glassy eye on the shelf,
woven in the web of notes that sprays from a trumpet,
announced by a salvo of crackles when the fire kindles,
printed on the nature of things when a skin bruises.

And there's never enough surprise at the killer in the self,
nor enough difference between the shooter and the shot,
nor enough melting down of stubs to make new candles
as the earth rolls over, inverting billions of houses.

MONA VAN DUYN

THE BURGLAR

Being a burglar, you slip out of doors in the morning
And look at the street by looking at the sky,
Not being taken in by anything blue.
You must look to the left or right to see across.
If nothing strikes your eye, if no one comes running,
You've stolen another day.

You must spend it on your toes
At the edges of buildings, doorways, and windows
Wherever no one is watching close enough.
Keep your fingers light as smoke.
You may have permission to kiss with one eye open.
Try every door while leaning away from it.

But sundown is serious; it's time to go home
To the house that will draw you under its empty wing.
Climbing like ivy up the drains, go through
The furthest window into a dark room.
Wait there to hear how everything has gone.
Then, masking every motion,

Glide to the stairwell.
They will be eating dinner: the man and the woman
At opposite ends of a white and silver table;
Between them, food and candles and children.
Their knives and forks go in and out of their mouths;

Whatever they do will aim them toward each other.
Now, follow your fingerprints around all corners
From nightlatch to velvet lid, from hasp to stone.
Everything locked, of course, has been locked for **you**:
You must break in softly, take whatever you find
Whether you understand what it is or not.
Breathe in, reach out,

Stealing one gift at a time.
If you grow hungry, thinking of their desserts,
It's time to vanish over the windowsill.
You must go without their dinner into the night,
Not saying goodbye, not waiting to scrawl a note
To say you're running away, but running away.

DAVID WAGONER

SLEEPING BY A RIVER

My feet cut off from me, the ends of my legs
As heavy as the stones they're lying on,
One hand cupped empty over my forehead,
I wake by the riverside, catching myself
Napping, open-mouthed under a cloud.

A rock stuck in my back like a revolver
Holds me up a moment, lets me down
To this numb heap of matter
Whose pieces won't rouse out. I should have known
Better than this. There isn't one dumb creature

Back in the woods who'd fall asleep out here.
There's too much give and take out in the open.
Someone moved the sun when I wasn't looking
And did me to a turn as red as leaves.
Here come the flies across the hatch of evening.

And something drank my spirits while I slept,
Then corked me like a bottle without a message.
It coaxed the soul out of my fingertips,
Spun out its prints as vaguely as whirlpools,
Rippled across my forehead, and flew off.

I shift my upper eye to see the crows
Leaving an alder, full of their dark selves.
This is the way it goes.
The soul goes straight away as the crow flies
With enough noise to wake what's left behind
And leave it, one eye up, like a dying salmon.

DAVID WAGONER

SPEECH FROM A COMEDY

(Scene: The wreckage of Heaven)

I am God. But all my creatures are unkind to me.
They think of themselves. Why don't they think of me?
I'm holier than they.
    (Chorus) God is lovely.
If I descended and rode through the streets,
Would they take off their hats?
No, they'd keep their hands in each other's pockets.
    (Chorus) God is out of sorts.
Or if I showed up to give a formal address
Including an enormous amount of sound, godly advice,
They'd turn and wriggle away like a school of fish.
    (Chorus) God is endless.
I burned myself in a bush once. Day and night,
I burned like a pillar of virtue in the desert.
I even let them watch me ride in my chariot.
    (Chorus) God is great.
I gave them Aaron's rod when they were on the rocks.
I plagued their enemies with a thousand dirty tricks.
I let them burn rams in thickets instead of their precious
    Isaacs.
    (Chorus) God is on their backs.
When things looked so black they couldn't tell his from hers,
I parted the waters,
Saving a few. But drowning a lot of others.
    (Chorus) God is feeling worse.
Didn't I die for them?
Hang myself? And shed the Blood of the Lamb?
What more could I do? Try it yourself sometime.
    (Chorus) God is sublime.
Now they forsake me. Leave me up in the air.
Sinning. Thinking of pleasure.
The more I leave them alone, the worse they are.
    (Chorus) God is pure.

126

They lie all night in their houses stacked in rows,
Their knees pulled up, their heads stuffed into pillows,
Imagining new ways to break my laws.
>(*Chorus*) God is jealous.
When I show them a bad example, plastered and confused,
Chances are he'll be headlined and idolized.
The only law of mine they like is getting circumcised.
>(*Chorus*) God is not amused.
I didn't ask for anything impossible.
I said, "Love me—and not just once in a while."
But all men were created fickle.
>(*Chorus*) God is immortal.
I'll settle with Everyman.
I had his dinner all laid out in my mansion,
But *he* had to try cooking his *own*.
>(*Chorus*) God is burning.
Just because angels are blasé and neuter,
Did he think I'd be contented forever and ever
Playing with Ezekiel's wheel or climbing up and down Jacob's
ladder?
>(*Chorus*) God is boiling over.
I made him in my image, didn't I?
I gave him my tooth for a tooth, my eye for an eye.
How could I turn out such an unreasonable facsimile?
>(*Chorus*) God is mighty sorry.
He'll be made to see the way things really are.
If he's so fond of slaughter,
I can get it for him wholesale just by losing my temper.
>(*Chorus*) God's a man-of-war.
I might have shown him mercy,
But nobody asked me.
The best things in Heaven are costly.
>(*Chorus*) God is free.
All right, he's dug his bed. Now let him lie in it
A thousand years at a stretch on a strict diet
While worms with their noses on fire pay an endless visit.
>(*Chorus*) God is like that.

I watched over him like a shepherd over a sheep
While he went bleating and gambolling and flocking around
     and getting fleeced, forgetting whom to worship.
Well, every shepherd knows his way to the butchershop.
     (*Chorus*) God is in bad shape.
Come, Death. He has made me mad.
I summon Death. For his ingratitude,
Everyman must choke on his daily bread.
     (*Chorus*) God is sick and tired.

DAVID WAGONER

THE SHOOTING OF JOHN DILLINGER OUTSIDE THE BIOGRAPH THEATER, JULY 22, 1934

Chicago ran a fever of a hundred and one that groggy Sunday.
A reporter fried an egg on a sidewalk; the air looked shaky.
And a hundred thousand people were in the lake like shirts
    in a laundry.
Why was Johnny lonely?
Not because two dozen solid citizens, heat-struck, had
    keeled over backward.
Not because those lawful souls had fallen out of their sockets
    and melted.
But because the sun went down like a lump in a furnace or
    a bull in the Stockyards.
Where was Johnny headed?
Under the Biograph Theater sign that said, "Our Air is
    Refrigerated,"
Past seventeen FBI men and four policemen who stood in
    doorways and sweated.
Johnny sat down in a cold seat to watch Clark Gable get
    electrocuted.
Had Johnny been mistreated?
Yes, but Gable told the D.A. he'd rather fry than be shut up
    forever.
Two women sat by Johnny. One looked sweet, one looked
    like J. Edgar Hoover.
Polly Hamilton made him feel hot, but Anna Sage made him
    shiver.
Was Johnny a good lover?
Yes, but he passed out his share of squeezes and pokes like a
    jittery masher
While Agent Purvis sneaked up and down the aisle like an
    extra usher,
Trying to make sure they wouldn't slip out till the show was
    over.
Was Johnny a fourflusher?
No, not if he knew the game. He got it up or got it back.

But he liked to take snapshots of policemen with his own
    Kodak,
And once in a while he liked to take them with an automatic.
Why was Johnny frantic?
Because he couldn't take a walk or sit down in a movie
Without being afraid he'd run smack into somebody
Who'd point at his rearranged face and holler, "Johnny!"
Was Johnny ugly?
Yes, because Dr. Wilhelm Loeser had given him a new profile
With a baggy jawline and squint eyes and an erased dimple,
With kangaroo-tendon cheekbones and a gigolo's mustache
    that should've been illegal.
Did Johnny love a girl?
Yes, a good-looking, hard-headed Indian named Billie
    Frechette.
He wanted to marry her and lie down and try to get over it,
But she was locked in jail for giving him first-aid and comfort.
Did Johnny feel hurt?
He felt like breaking a bank or jumping over a railing
Into some panicky teller's cage to shout, "Reach for the
    ceiling!"
Or like kicking some vice president in the bum checks and
    smiling.
What was he really doing?
Going up the aisle with the crowd and into the lobby
With Polly saying, "Would *you* do what Clark done?" And
    Johnny saying, "Maybe."
And Anna saying, "If he'd been smart, he'd of acted like
    Bing Crosby."
Did Johnny look flashy?
Yes, his white-on-white shirt and tie were luminous.
His trousers were creased like knives to the tops of his shoes,
And his yellow straw hat came down to his dark glasses.
Was Johnny suspicious?
Yes, and when Agent Purvis signalled with a trembling cigar,
Johnny ducked left and ran out of the theater,
And innocent Polly and squealing Anna were left nowhere.
Was Johnny a fast runner?
No, but he crouched and scurried past a friendly liquor store
Under the coupled arms of double-daters, under awnings,
    under stars,

To the curb at the mouth of an alley. He hunched there.
Was Johnny a thinker?
No, but he was thinking more or less of Billie Frechette
Who was lost in prison for longer than he could possibly wait,
And then it was suddenly too hard to think around a bullet.
Did anyone shoot straight?
Yes, but Mrs. Etta Natalsky fell out from under her picture
    hat.
Theresa Paulus sprawled on the sidewalk, clutching her left
    foot.
And both of them groaned loud and long under the streetlight.
Did Johnny like that?
No, but he lay down with those strange women, his face in
    the alley,
One shoe off, cinders in his mouth, his eyelids heavy.
When they shouted questions at him, he talked back to
    nobody.
Did Johnny lie easy?
Yes, holding his gun and holding his breath as a last trick,
He waited, but when the Agents came close, his breath
    wouldn't work.
Clark Gable walked his last mile; Johnny ran half a block.
Did he run out of luck?
Yes, before he was cool, they had him spread out on
    dished-in marble
In the Cook County Morgue, surrounded by babbling people
With a crime reporter presiding over the head of the table.
Did Johnny have a soul?
Yes, and it was climbing his slippery wind-pipe like a
    trapped burglar.
It was beating the inside of his ribcage, hollering, "Let me
    out of here!"
Maybe it got out, and maybe it just stayed there.
Was Johnny a money-maker?
Yes, and thousands paid 25¢ to see him, mostly women,
And one said, "I wouldn't have come, except he's a moral
    lesson,"
And another, "I'm disappointed. He feels like a dead man."
Did Johnny have a brain?
Yes, and it always worked best through the worst of dangers,
Through flat-footed hammerlocks, through guarded doors,
    around corners,

But it got taken out in the morgue and sold to some doctors.
Could Johnny take orders?
No, but he stayed in the wicker basket carried by six men
Through the bulging crowd to the hearse and let himself be
    locked in,
And he stayed put as it went driving south in a driving rain.
And he didn't get stolen?
No, not even after his old hard-nosed dad refused to sell
The quick-drawing corpse for $10,000 to somebody in a
    carnival.
He figured he'd let *Johnny* decide how to get to Hell.
Did anyone wish him well?
Yes, half of Indiana camped in the family pasture,
And the minister said, "With luck, he could have been a
    minister."
And up the sleeve of his oversized gray suit, Johnny twitched
    a finger.
Does anyone remember?
Everyone still alive. And some dead ones. It was a new kind
    of holiday
With hot and cold drinks and hot and cold tears. They
    planted him in a cemetery
With three unknown vice presidents, Benjamin Harrison,
    and James Whitcomb Riley,
Who never held up anybody.

DAVID WAGONER

AFTER FEVER

Late the third night, it was, the fever lifted.
I felt composure fall like heavy velours,
fold, fold upon fold, until the room was filled.

Unaware once more of taking any breath,
I wiped my breath away from the misted glass
to watch my image outside in the darkness

staring steadily back across the stillness
and into the swaddled air. Here, hours before,
counting each gasp and desperate fingerhold

three hundred feet above a slithering sea,
I clawed the greasy tiles of a sloping roof
and then was launched in a vivifying wind

to learn how easeful falling through water is.
Endlessly, endlessly, cushioned on the plush
that covered what seemed like comfortable death,

I felt myself fall till I sensed that the sea
was not sea, nor wind wind, nor this death my death;
and the notion, like my image, vanishing

with the nap of dark in the beginning day,
left me standing cold to breathe by a window,
watching the world, unstifled with common wind,

shuffling back like an aging adulterer,
traipsing shabbily back through the fallen leaves
and up to my door as if nothing had happened.

TED WALKER

APOCALYPSE ON THE JETTY

Weather-rucked, intermittent
in the jetty's starboard light,
the faces of the codling men,
grim, furred with frost, intent,
clamp upon the coming night.

After the last, curling cast,
they trim their tackle, settle
themselves to the searchless lust
that clings to them after a kill.
As the tide slackens, and the shoal

moves on, they know their need.
When day shelves, before full dark
they drowse to cold in shallows
deep enough to dream in, where they
drift, bait for the want that swallows

them, strafing, as a seeking shark
sucks mullet. January
lifts no lid. They will not wake,
though ice prise open an eye,
before sleep unbars one glimpse

of that long, white-ribbed corridor,
fragrant with wax of ambergris,
and lit with pins of phosphor
where, willing Jonahs, alone
beyond all ends of ocean,

they would wish to walk in calm,
their shriek left in the gull's tough jaw.
And, before some morning wakener
lifts their welded fingers from
the tightening grip of their dream—

before they stamp back warmth and fear
to suffuse their bodies once more,
and they return, shivering, home
from the sea's ascendancy
so nearly shared—they will have seen

fragments enough of a vision
that will surely bring them back,
failing, where they will fail again,
to court the comfortable cold
a man might gently die in.

TED WALKER

BIRTHDAY SONG

With winds that strop on little stones
Beside the water's open throat,
A steel November birthday hones
The rusted scissors of the thought
That I am thirty and that I
Have yet to see somebody die.

Had I but asked, when I was young,
To touch my sister's hardened hand,
(That three-week sister with one lung,
Whose life I could not comprehend),
I may have learned to look on death
As triumph in the fight for breath:

Or if, successive mournings since,
I'd seen a misted mirror clear,
Perhaps my mind could countenance
That life is all we have to fear,
Believing lips set in repose
Suggest far less than I suppose.

For, walking where the river's lip
Is wiped by willows that entwine,
Recalling coffin-slings that slip
Through knuckles knowing more than mine,
I look behind my silent tread
And blink as, level with my head,

My birthday morning mints a sun—
A coin to double-lid an eye
That might, before I'm thirty-one,
Secure the image lastingly
Of how a loved one did not look
Before the last time she awoke.

TED WALKER

BLOW, WEST WIND

I know, I know—though the evidence
Is lost, and the last who might speak are dead.
Blow, west wind, blow, for the evidence, O,

Is lost, and wind shakes the cedar, and O,
I know how the kestrel hung over Wyoming,
Breast reddened in sunset, and O, the cedar

Shakes, and I know how cold
Was the sweat on my father's mouth, dead.
Blow, west wind, blow, shake the cedar, I know

How once I, a boy, crouching at creekside,
Watched, in the sunlight, a handful of water
Drip, drip, from my hand. The drops—they
    were bright!

But you believe nothing, the evidence lost.

ROBERT PENN WARREN

DIGGING THE PAST

1

Here, then,
Where waters spin
Fleeing from men
Round quartz and spar,
The rock shelves in,
Opening the cave mouth, far
Above the waves' morass of seaweed, sticks and tar.

Gulls crying
Pure anguish now,
This, that way flying,
Swoop, stall, proclaim
In trespass how
Under their nests we came
To read such hieroglyphs as give the void a name.

Foot-crossed,
The limestone bridge
Lets fall the tossed
Waves with a roar.
From ridge to ridge
Of rock we go before;
Then the receding tide behind us locks the door.

We crouch,
As though a hand
Of kindred touch
Almost in reach,
Knowing our planned
Spadework, laid hold on each,
Or finger signed us dumb, to hear forgotten speech.

Fires fling
Shades on the wall,
Flicker and cling
To earth, being made
By man. Birds call.
White wings on water fade,
And seething waves rush up, swift to consume the
    shade.

2

Too deep inside ourselves
Lies Elsinore.
Where weapons shone,
Stubborn ore,
Danegeld of our attention
Leaps to the muscles' tension
As the spade delves.

While the gymnastic shade
Compasses effort
To track pierced veins,
Rock's retort
Answers the shoulders' strains.
Fossil of mole remains;
The ghost is laid.

Still we persist, to extract
Bone or ceramic,
Glazed by unseeing
Cataract, then quick
With vision's vital spring.
We stoop to break time's ring
And show clear fact.

Without this toil no city
Finds equilibrium;
No foil discovers
Quick and dumb,
Nor forty thousand brothers
Time's truth, where one grave smothers
Identity.

Still the rock's reticence
Pulls our awareness
Downward, to ease
The forbears' stress
Of soul, till mindstrength frees
Those inmost rarities,
True and intense.

3

Impulsive invader, the wave from the gully now fills the whole
    seacave, feeling
Nothing of mind in the sleek black walls, no singular touch
    or caress.
One wave racing back calls another that hurls the white
    spray to the ceiling,
Subduing with trumpets of sea all that lived in the cavern's
    recess.

So the light-headed spray thrown back from the breakers
    reports what is not for man's knowing;
Yet I, who enter above them, ignored by their deafening crash,
In the thunder and conflict of waves, and of waters endlessly
    flowing,
Find peace in man's counter-wave music, rejecting their
    turmoil as trash.

4

In the cave's mouth, not far from the headland, breaking
Red clay stacked near stalagmites built by tears,
A dome darkened, unentered thousands of years,
Our fingers grope and sift,
While pick strikes, to break rock they cannot lift,
To ease the rift
Of forms embedded too fast to expect this waking.

And yet how fresh in shadow, under the pressure
Of shredding fingers, white in friable mould
As primrose under dark leaf, emerges cold
This that reveals its own
Fragile form, a clay-stemmed antelope's bone
Fluting to stone
A vanishing note as hunters enter the fissure.

Far under, that breathing monster nuzzles the shady
Steep cliff at the height of summer's tide.
Look up. Forget the youth mistaken for bride
In ochre. Salute the strong
Tang of seaweed, driftwood, spangle and thong:
Never so long
A wake sighed, as for Paviland's Red Lady.

Life returns to the mother; and she, the daughter,
Knows in the desert what gentler touch is here,
Crumbling, close to that pendant worn in the ear
Found in yesterday's stint.
Bone whitens, quickly distinguished from flint,
Like flesh, the print
Of all that eludes and is different, thirsting for water.

NOTE: The Red Lady of Paviland, the name given to the earliest skeleton un-
earthed in Britain, because of red ochre rock deposits mistaken for ritual dyes,
was first thought to be the skeleton of a girl, but was later identified as that of
a youth of about eighteen.

VERNON WATKINS

TO A SHELL

At last, beautiful shell,
Lie there crushed; but the sea
Cannot obliterate yet
Faith I remember well:
A house facing the sea.
Hard and bitterly
Though waves beat on that wall
From the swirling quicksands of debt,
I swear that it cannot fall.

Nor can you drag those words,
Confident in their day,
Down to the unknown deep.
I have a net whose cords
Gather the fallen day
And make the forgotten stay
In all but the detail death
Moves to the realm of sleep,
So strong is the pledge of breath.

And though the magical dice,
Loaded for nothing, toss
All to perdition, left
In darkness, held in a vice,
No white breaker can toss
All to a total loss.
Still the relic will hold,
Caught in a secret cleft,
Tenderer light than gold.

All I remember, all
Of the locked, unfolding days
Where to-morrow's treasure shines.
Fragile nautilus caul,
Tell the fingers of days:
"Find me. Enter the praise
Of Eden's morning, inlaid
With dazzling, intimate lines.
Touch, and the world will fade."

VERNON WATKINS

AMAGANSETT BEACH REVISITED

I

Once more I move among you, dear familiar places,
Pale shores, pale dunes, long burdened by my long love
    of you—
The sun strikes the great glass of ocean a glancing blow,
The waves are kneeling in the sun-dazzled spaces.
June is upon us: earth and sea
Are thronged with tidal life; the mackerel now
Swarm the Atlantic shallows; from some bough
Inland, the red-winged blackbird sounds his
    "fleur-de-lis"—
Life, that lifts up
In the green woodland the day-lily's cup,
Wakes in my heart once more;
Imagination spreads wide wings in me.
The blue road of the sea,
The void sea-road that runs
From here to the horizon, now—as once
In earlier summers when I strode along,
Measuring to the sea's rhythm the rhythms of
    my song—
Beckons imagination on.

II

All afternoon, I have pressed
Eastward, toward Amagansett. In the west,
The sun grazes the rim. Two sandpipers
Companion me now along the way—
They skirt the surges, keeping just out of reach
Of the advancing and receding foam.
It is early evening; we have come
To the broad shelf of Amagansett beach.
In the enormous dome
Seaward, the horizon is garlanded
With tender clouds; the hollow shell
Of heaven is luminous; the exhausted, pale
Waters exhale
A vast oceanic odor, a sea-soft breath.
Sundown. A sense of absence and of vacancy.
While there is still daylight,
A faint moon-path appears upon the sea;
While yet the living light prevails
Against the encroaching night,
The tenuous light of memory
Sets its cold seal upon
All that is gone—
On the now vanished day,
On the now vanished past.

JOHN HALL WHEELOCK

THE MOVEMENTS OF BOYS

They come in from the outside
like slow arrows upright
and circle, looking.

But only look at *things*.
Their eyes never meet
the eyes of people,

who are not there, for them.
They touch things sometimes,
moving without speech,

and ceremoniously.
But what their gestures mean
remains a cult, unknown

to anyone but them.
A hint of catalepsy
a hint of pure religion:

ritual, a pagan
touching of a source
animal, inhuman.

Their eyes are vague, opaque,
oblong, like a soapstone
or ocean color

rejecting light and feeling.
Their hair is dark blond
falling long for boys:

they are as strange as gods
from ancient, thicker seasons,
graceful, uninvaded,

or are the human type
to come—a signal like a drum
we hear but cannot see.

JOAN WHITE

THE HAWK

tilted while we sat still,
theoretic thing,
and streaked, bent tense to kill
on pointed wing—

what was a feathered cross
cruising admired in skies
became what we knew of hawks—
a clawed surprise

to tear whatever it was—
lamb tottering lost
or rabbit hopping in grass—
some gentleness,

as if nature had meant
to demonstrate by this
bird with a low intent,
its deadly purpose—

how meekness hasn't a chance
under the eye of power,
the high, wide cateyed glance
and hookbeak glower

of a hawk or anything else
so well equipped
with plumages of stealth,
sharply tipped.

So we thought as we watched
the hawk swoop down—
nothing is safe that's soft
or slow on the ground,

yet we had food for thought
when the hawk flapped up again—
tenderness hadn't been caught.
It blended in.

HAROLD WITT

Date Due

PRINTED IN U.S.A.